INTERFACES

Series Editor: Barbara Green, O.P.

Dining with Pharisees

J. Patrick Mullen

A Michael Glazier Book

LITURGICAL PRESS

Collegeville, Minnesota

www.litpress.org

A Michael Glazier Book published by the Liturgical Press

Cover design by Ann Blattner. Watercolor by Ethel Boyle.

Unless otherwise noted, the Scripture quotations are translations by the author from the Greek text.

1	2	3	4	5	6	7	8	9

Library of Congress Cataloging-in-Publication Data

Mullen, J. Patrick
    Dining with Pharisees / J. Patrick Mullen.
      p. cm. — (An interfaces book)
    "A Michael Glazier book."
    Includes bibliographical references.
    ISBN 0-8146-5162-3
    1. Pharisees. 2. Simon, the Pharisee. 3. Jews in the New Testament. 4. Bible N.T. Luke VII, 36–50—Criticism, Redaction. 5. Bible. N.T. Luke VII, 36–50 —Social scientific criticism. I. Title. II. Series: Interfaces (Collegeville, Minn.).

BS2595.6.J44M85   2004
226.4'06—dc22

                                                          2004002933

CONTENTS

PREFACE

The book you hold in your hand is one of ten volumes in a new set. This series, called INTERFACES, is basically a curriculum adventure, a creative opportunity in teaching and learning, presented at this moment in the long story of how the Bible has been studied, interpreted, and appropriated.

The INTERFACES project was prompted by a number of experiences that you, perhaps, share. When I first taught undergraduates, the college had just received a substantial grant from the National Endowment for the Humanities, and one of the recurring courses designed within the grant was called Great Figures in Pursuit of Excellence. Three courses would be taught, each centering on a figure from some academic discipline, with a common seminar section to provide occasion for some integration. Some triads were more successful than others, as you might imagine. But the opportunity to concentrate on a single individual—whether historical or literary—to team teach, to make links to another pair of figures, and to learn new things about other disciplines was stimulating and fun for all involved. A second experience that gave rise to the present series came at the same time, connected as well with undergraduates. It was my frequent experience to have Roman Catholic students feel quite put out about taking "more" biblical studies, since, as they confidently affirmed, they had already been there many times and done it all. That was, of course, not true; as we well know, there is always more to learn. And often those who felt most informed were the least likely to take on new information when offered it.

A stimulus as primary as my experience with students was the familiarity of listening to friends and colleagues at professional meetings talking about the research that excites us most. I often wondered: Do her undergraduate students know about this? Or how does he bring these ideas—clearly so energizing to him—into the college classroom? Perhaps some of us have felt bored with classes that seem wholly unrelated to research, that rehash the same familiar material repeatedly. Hence the idea for this series of books to bring to the fore and combine some of our research interests with our teaching and learning. Accordingly, this series is not so much about creating texts *for* student audiences but rather about *sharing* our scholarly passions with them. Because these volumes are intended each as a piece of original scholarship, they are geared to be stimulating to both students and established scholars, perhaps resulting in some fruitful collaborative learning adventures.

The series also developed from a widely shared sense that all academic fields are expanding and exploding, and that to contemplate "covering" even a testament (let alone the whole Bible or Western monotheistic religions) needs to be abandoned in favor of something with greater depth and fresh focus. At the same time, the links between our fields are becoming increasingly obvious as well, and the possibilities for study that draw together academic realms that had once seemed separate is exciting. Finally, the spark of enthusiasm that almost always ignited when I mentioned to students and colleagues the idea of single figures in combination—interfacing—encouraged me that this was an idea worth trying.

And so with the leadership and help of Liturgical Press Academic Editor Linda Maloney, as well as with the encouragement and support of Editorial Director Mark Twomey, the series has begun to take shape.

Each volume in the INTERFACES series focuses clearly on a biblical character (or perhaps a pair of them). The characters from the first set of volumes are in some cases powerful—King Saul, Pontius Pilate—and familiar—John the Baptist, the patriarch Joseph; in other cases they will strike you as minor and little-known—the Cannibal Mothers, Herodias. The second "litter" emerging adds notables of various ranks and classes: Jezebel, queen of the Northern Israelite realm; James of Jerusalem, "brother of the Lord"; Simon the Pharisee, dinner host to Jesus; Legion, the Gerasene demoniac encountered so dramatically by Jesus. In any case, each of them has been chosen to open up a set of worlds for consideration. The named (or unnamed) character interfaces with his or her historical-cultural world and its many issues, with other characters from biblical literature; each character has drawn forth the creativity of the author, who has taken on the challenge of engaging many readers. The books are designed for college students (though we think they are suitable for seminary courses and for serious Bible study), planned to provide young adults with relevant information and at a level of critical sophistication that matches the rest of the undergraduate curriculum. In fact, the expectation is that what students are learning of historiography, literary theory, and cultural anthropology in other classes will find an echo in these books, each of which is explicit about at least two relevant methodologies. It is surely the case that biblical studies is in a methodology-conscious moment, and the INTERFACES series embraces it enthusiastically. Our hope is for students to continue to see the relationship between their best questions and their most valuable insights, between how they approach texts and what they find there. The volumes go well beyond familiar paraphrase of narratives to ask questions that are relevant in our era. At the same time, the series authors also have each dealt with the notion of the Bible as Scripture in a way condign for them. None of the books is preachy or hortatory, and yet the self-implicating aspects of working with the revelatory text are handled frankly. The assumption is, again, that college can be a good time for people to reexamine and rethink their beliefs and assumptions, and they need to do so in good company. The INTERFACES volumes all challenge teachers to re-vision radically the scope of a course, to allow the many connections among characters to serve as its warp and weft. What would emerge fresh if a Deuteronomistic History class were organized around King Saul, Queen Jezebel, and the two women who petitioned their nameless monarch? How is Jesus' ministry thrown into fresh relief when structured by shared concerns implied by a demoniac, a Pharisee, James—a disciple, and John the Baptist—a mentor? And for those who must "do it all" in one semester, a study of Genesis' Joseph, Herodias, and Pontius Pilate might allow for a timely foray into postcolonialism.

The INTERFACES volumes are not substitutes for the Bible. In every case they are to be read with the text. Quoting has been kept to a minimum for that very reason. The series is accompanied by a straightforward companion, *From Earth's Creation to John's Revelation: The INTERFACES Biblical Storyline Companion,* which provides a quick overview of the whole storyline into which the characters under special study fit. The companion is available gratis for those using two or more of the INTERFACES volumes. Already readers of diverse proficiency and familiarity have registered satisfaction with this slim overview narrated by biblical Sophia.

The series' challenge—for publisher, writers, teachers, and students—is to combine the volumes creatively, to INTERFACE them well so that the vast potential of the biblical text continues to unfold for us all. These ten volumes offer a foretaste of other volumes currently on the drawing board. It has been a pleasure to work with the authors of these first volumes as well as with the series consultants: Carleen Mandolfo for Hebrew Bible and Catherine Murphy for New Testament. It is the hope of all of us that you will find the series useful and stimulating for your own teaching and learning.

Barbara Green, O.P.
INTERFACES Series Editor
May 16, 2004
Berkeley, California

INTRODUCTION

Composition and Theological Nuance:
Redaction Criticism

This book is essentially about the interfacing of contexts. All stories, even those told of historical events, have a number of contexts, including, among others, the world within the story, the world of the author, and the world of the reader. These worlds inevitably intersect and affect each other, creating alternative meanings from what would have been understood by the original participants in the stories recorded. Authors create or report narratives they conceive of as coherent according to their own standards. Readers, necessarily, interpret the world of the story within the framework of what they already know and with which they are familiar. For example, J.R.R. Tolkien's *The Lord of the Rings* is understood by modern readers as fantasy, but if told by an eighth-century Norse bard to his contemporaries might receive a completely different reception as an expression of their mythic, religious, and yet *true* past. Thus there may be more than one way of interpreting a given narrative. Those who participate in an incident may understand it one way while those who witnessed it, remembered it, and passed it on or made a record of it may have another, and those who later read about it yet others.

As a reflection of this, in addition to the cultural questions, an observant reader will note that there are both similarities and differences between the account of the anointing of Jesus in Luke 7:36-50 and parallel incidents recorded in the other three gospels, Mark 14:3-9, Matthew 26:6-13, and John 12:1-8. It would be good to read each of these episodes at this point, while considering how similar and divergent they are. How do we explain the similarities between these accounts? Are they all rooted in some common event or story, and if so, why do they vary so much? Why are the issues of the expense of the ointment and the needs of the poor, the heart of the controversy in the versions found in Matthew, Mark, and John, not addressed at all in Luke? Why are the questions of love and forgiveness, so prominent in Luke's version, absent from the other gospels' versions? Why is Luke's version placed toward the beginning of his gospel while the other three place it at the end? If we determine that the woman in Luke's version is a prostitute because of her behavior, does that mean we should draw the same conclusion of Mary of Bethany in John's story?

Again, to reveal my hand a bit, if we accept, as do the great majority of biblical scholars, that Mark was the earliest gospel and that Luke used Mark's text as a foundation for the composition of his much longer gospel, points we will take up later, then it is curious that Luke would have a story so similar to one in Mark and yet at a completely different place in the storyline, with such radically different discussions about the meaning of the woman's character and behavior.

The process of studying the alteration of earlier texts by later writers is called "redaction criticism." The motivation for this technique is curiosity. What motivated Luke to alter Mark's original tale? What clues does this give us to Luke's personality, his theological agenda, his dissatisfaction with Mark's version, his audience and their needs? The answers to these questions sometimes give us keys to the cultural backgrounds of the participants in the production of the texts. Identifying the cultural background of the authors then, in turn, gives us a key into yet deeper understanding of the pressures, concerns, and insights of the readership to which the authors are responding, since authors usually do not work in a vacuum. The gospel writers, and Luke no less than the others, were writing for a purpose, presumably to teach and challenge, to enlighten and encourage a specific audience, responding to their religious needs as people embedded in a unique culture.

Questions of Behavior and Culture:
Anthropology and Scripture

Many people who travel to foreign lands or interact with immigrants from other countries stumble innocently, misunderstanding the meanings of foreign words and phrases, gestures, and customs. I remember once being asked by an American of European extraction my impressions of a young man we both knew. I responded that he reminded me of a "puppy." By this I meant that he was a nice, well-intentioned, bouncy kind of fellow, but that every now and then someone needed "to spread some newspapers," if you catch my drift. He was known to get himself into lots of little scrapes and cause mini-crises for others because of his enthusiasm for life and his lack of either experience or common sense. He did, however, almost always mean well. I used "puppy" as a sort of summary of all of this. Unfortunately a Mexican acquaintance, whose knowledge of American culture was limited, overheard my remark and was offended. He translated "puppy" into Spanish as *perito,* or "little dog," a highly offensive term to use about another in his culture. *Perito* failed to communicate the intent of my evaluation of the young man in any sense.

These misunderstandings even happen with people who speak the same language, as do Americans and the British. It has been said that they are two peoples "separated by a common language." For example, a "boot" in America is a big, hard-duty kind of foot apparel, whereas among the British it's what Americans refer to as the "trunk" of the car. We can see that even when conversation is held between people who share a common language it doesn't always mean that accurate communication and understanding occur.

Cross-cultural communication is further hampered, even when there is a common language, since spoken and written words are only one way in which we communicate. Subtle communications are passed between people by body posture, proximity, gestures, facial expressions, clothing, jewelry, and even pronunciation. Sometimes only local "insiders" can successfully interpret some of the finer points of these communications. This much larger world of meanings, accompanied and supported by shared understandings of appropriate social relationships, are expressions of "culture." As a result, eating Mexican food and knowing how to speak Spanish may bring people from the United States into contact with people from Mexico and allow them to interact with them, but it does *not* make those from the north sensitive to and conversant with the rich world of meanings shaped by the artistic and religious expressions, historical roots, economic and political realities, family structures, gender roles and the like that make up the Mexican culture, let alone the unique expression of that culture as found, say, only in Sinaloa, Mexico.

When we encounter literature from other cultures, times, and places, the problem can be acute. The Bible, though a familiar text to many in the twenty-first century, was composed by members of societies that ceased to exist so long ago and at such a geographical remove that it would be a wonder if it wasn't subject to cultural misunderstanding. We need to consider whether our cultural separation from that ancient world leads to misapprehension and even misinterpretations of the meanings of the biblical texts. To highlight this question, this book will investigate the passage mentioned above, the meal from Luke 7:36-50, wherein Jesus is the invited guest at the house of Simon, a Pharisee, somewhere in Palestine, in the early mid-first century.

In what appears to be a simple story set in the Semitic, Judean, and peasant world of an itinerant preacher, Jesus, and a Pharisee, Simon, we have many cultural questions to consider. Even if you have a general idea of the overall content of Luke 7:36-50, it would be beneficial to read it again at this point while considering the following questions: Does this story reflect typical behavior from my own culture, the rural Judean culture about which it writes, or the urban Hellenistic world of the writer, Luke? How fair is the portrayal of Simon as a Pharisee? What evidence is there of Simon's place in the world? How influential was he? What kind of hospitality was appropriate and to be expected? What religious aspirations motivated Simon's invitation to Jesus in the first place? Is the host a hostile opponent to Jesus or a genial and hopeful enquirer? What manner of meal is this, wherein men recline and eat and women, who do not eat, wander in uninvited? What does it mean for a woman to be present at a meal, or for her to be crying, or for her to touch the feet of a man not her husband? Is the weeping woman a prostitute or not, and why is she silent? Does this story present a positive or negative message for women? Is forgiveness a result of great love, or its cause?

Perhaps you may be acknowledging that you don't know the answer to several of these questions. That would be a *good* start! On the other hand, you may well be tempted, in fact it would be natural, to answer all of these questions according to your own lived experience of the meaning of words and actions, according to your own place and culture of origins. Allow me to reveal my hand (a reference to card playing that would make absolutely no sense to someone from Simon's world) by saying that it would be a mistake to fill in the gaps with, "Well, if this had happened at *my* house then the answer to the questions would be. . . ." This book will ask what the answers would have been for Jesus and Simon according to *their* worldview, and for Luke and Luke's audience according to *theirs.* We may not have sufficient information to answer all of our questions, but that in itself is useful. Recognizing what you don't know is an important preliminary step in deciding *not* to speak with undeserved confidence or in error.

Because Simon plays such an important role, prompting the meal, drawing conclusions, and interacting with Jesus as a Pharisee, it is clear that understanding the Pharisees is an essential step in addressing some of these questions. Pharisees play crucial roles in narratives throughout the New Testament, asking questions, testing Jesus, forming associations, planning, and plotting. These narrative roles may have been based on historical events or they may result from the creative work of the evangelists. It is worth considering from the start whether the evangelists' portrayal was unbiased. We may well ask whether an objective, historical portrayal of Jesus' opponents was a priority for the gospel writers. Could it be that

Pharisees served simply as foils, whose actions provide opportunities for Jesus to act, and in particular to teach?

Our motives are different from those of the evangelists, however, and can include an awareness of how pejorative readings of Pharisaic belief and practice have affected Christian and Jewish relationships in our own world. We live shortly after a time when all of humanity paid an unspeakable price for anti-Semitism springing substantially from the portrayal and interpretation of the portrayal of Jews, and Pharisees in particular, in the New Testament. We need to understand that ancient world better, to explain it with greater clarity so that, if for no other reason, we may put an end to the persecutions and pogroms that have circumscribed Jewish life wherever the New Testament is influential. This compels us to reexamine the evidence, and where possible while remaining faithful to the text, to provide alternative understandings with less weighted results.

The only way to obtain any historical objectivity concerning the real world behind this passage, if that can be conceived of as a value, is to intentionally pursue understanding of the values and activities of the Pharisees without any unduly pejorative evaluations. The methods used in this book are being employed, in combination, for just that purpose.

Summary

This work will investigate the different worlds of Luke 7:36-50, the narrative of Jesus' encounter with the weeping woman at Simon's house, focusing on the perspectives of those who "participated," or as close to them as we can get, and those who finally recorded it. It will pursue two methodologies, redaction criticism and anthropology, both of which are concerned with issues of context, though from different angles. The ultimate purpose is to understand both the methodologies and, in this case, the narrative itself of Luke 7:36-50.

The first method is redaction criticism, which compares different versions of a narrative and focuses on authorial changes, seeking to uncover the final author's theological and narrative emphases. This enables the contemporary reader of Scripture to perceive what is unique in Luke's gospel. Rather than blending all the gospels into one indiscriminate portrayal, we can then take advantage of four unique perspectives on Jesus' life.

The second method is anthropology, a methodology particularly useful for considering the cultural worlds of the narrative, the author, and the reader, demonstrating how each can color and shade interpretation. In particular, this method will be used to reconstruct, as best we can within the severe historical constraints involved, Simon's Pharisaic cultural matrix and worldview and, with more brevity, Luke's Greco-Roman response to the traditions he received. This will allow the contemporary reader to see the many layers of understanding at play, and to pursue understandings other than the most comfortable variety that presume that everyone thinks and believes and acts the way that "I" or "we" do in our twenty-first century reader's perspective.

We will begin by explaining the two methodologies before actually addressing the text of Luke 7:36-50, since the methods very quickly begin to interface in the actual application. To engage in authentic cultural criticism of a text one must be aware of what culture is actually responsible for the text being studied. When studying a document with a history as complicated as Luke's gospel, determining who is responsible for the different elements of the text is, in itself, a convoluted task. At the same time, though, some of the keys to determining responsibility are the cultural details contained in the various layers of the final product of the text. In essence these two methods dovetail in the process of developing a deeper insight into the production and purpose of the texts in their original settings.

CHAPTER ONE

Redaction Criticism

The Formation of the Synoptic Gospels

1. *The Identity and Enterprise of the Evangelists: Editor and Creator*

It has long been recognized that the four gospels and Acts do not give identical portrayals of Jesus. They each have their own nuances, areas of interest, and unique insights into the person of Jesus and his companions. There are also significant differences between them in historical details, such as how Judas Iscariot dispensed with his thirty silver pieces and how he died,[1] or the timing of the cleansing of the Temple: Was it at the beginning of Jesus' ministry or at the end?[2] Such differences, and there are *many* such revealed by careful side-by-side analysis of the gospels, are more numerous and substantial than would result from the different perspectives of eyewitnesses. In fact, many Scripture scholars question whether any of the gospel authors was actually an eyewitness of the events recounted, or whether instead these writers were recipients of the testimony of others.

These variations pose difficulties for those who, often for reasons of faith, insist that, as inspired documents, the gospels are inerrant histories of the life of Jesus from eyewitnesses. They are hard-pressed to provide credible explanations for the differences, for example, suggesting that since Temple cleansings are portrayed at both the beginning and end of Jesus' life in the four gospels, the event must have happened twice. Such facile explanations seldom satisfy, and often lead to further questions: e.g.,

---

[1] Compare Matt 27:5; Acts 1:18.

[2] John places it at the beginning (2:13-17), whereas the other gospels place it at the end (Matt 21:12-13//Mark 11:15-17//Luke 19:45-46).

1

if the cleansing happened twice, why is it mentioned only once in each gospel?

Most scholars would hold that it is too simplistic to suggest that the four gospels are "histories" as commonly understood from a Euro-American twenty-first-century perspective. While we know that "histories" existed in the Ancient Near East, there were different standards for producing them in that time than the ones familiar to us. The requirement for faithful and literal transmission by unbiased eyewitnesses, a standard we find difficult to reach though we claim to aspire to it, were not stringently applied in the ancient world. Thucydides, for example, considered it appropriate for historians to write, when they were uncertain about the actual content of a speech, what *ought* to have been said, though sticking to the gist of things, for the sake of the edification of the audience.[3]

It should be remembered that Jesus was not followed by attentive scribes taking careful notes of his activities and words. It seems quite possible that Jesus' importance as an historical personage only dawned on his disciples relatively late in their shared life together. The gospels, Mark in particular, as you may recall, make it clear that the disciples often did not understand Jesus, his teachings, or his role as the Messiah.

Although literacy levels at the time are uncertain, it remains unlikely that any of the twelve apostles was sufficiently educated, with the possible exception of Matthew/Levi, the tax collector, to have made careful, written notations of Jesus' activities or teachings. On the other hand, authors did not actually need to take quill and papyrus in hand to compose their writings, since dictation was available. Paul was known to have dictated his material to scribes, as is clearly the case in Rom 16:22 where Tertius, a Christian scribe, inserted a personal note of greeting to the dictation he received from Paul.[4]

There are two gospels attributed to names shared by Jesus' apostles, Matthew and John, but the significance of this is debatable. The attribution of those names to those gospels was fairly late, in the early second century. We know that other such ascriptions by Christians in the first century were made because the writings were produced by communities associated with great figures, and even more awkwardly when it is probable that the ascribed "author" had virtually nothing to do with the text as written. Another problem is dating. Internal evidence in Mark, Matthew, and Luke suggests that the composers were aware of the Roman attack on Jerusalem

---

[3] Thucydides, *The Peloponnesian War,* ch. 22.

[4] After dictating the body of a document to a scribe, Paul was known to add a postscript to his letters in his "own hand," e.g., Phlm 19.

in 68–70 C.E.[5] The latter two seem to have been written some time after the city had actually fallen, further reducing the probability that the authors were contemporaries of Jesus.

It would seem that the best evidence suggests that Matthew, Mark, Luke, and John, the names by which we reference the actual evangelists, whatever names they really went by, were not eyewitnesses. If, then, their gospels correlate in any historical sense to the life of Jesus, the evangelists must have been the recipients of traditions passed down by earlier Christians, including those who observed Jesus' life. There is evidence in the texts that this more complex process included an intervening period of oral transmission, during which time stories and teachings were passed down by word of mouth from eyewitnesses to secondhand reporters, and then through second- and third-hand dissemination as well. Only then did chroniclers put them into written form, well after Jesus' life. As is the nature of oral transmission, the traditions themselves were likely flexible, subject to the memories and public speaking abilities of the orators, and shaped according to the pastoral needs and interests of the audience, as good public speakers do today. An oral stage of transmission can still be detected in the gospels, where we find lingering hints of mnemonic devices, such as use of link words and repeating patterns.[6] Eventually these stories were written down, though perhaps not, at least initially, in the form we received them today in the narratives of the gospels.

Consider the process you would have to undertake to chronicle the life of someone you knew well who has passed on, perhaps your grandmother. First you would have to assemble the events you thought were interesting enough for your intended audience and of value to them. You would probably have a mixture of materials, baptismal certificates, marriage licenses, or other documents recording important transitional events, typical things she used to say, stories she told you about her earlier years, events related to you by your parents, or your own indistinct childhood memories of her. As you began to assemble the details for inclusion in your biography you would likely find that some important details had been for-

[5] Mark 13; Matthew 24; Luke 21.

[6] For example, see Mark 9:47-50, the famous "If your eye offend you" passage, which ends by detailing the worm-ridden, fiery consequences for those who go to hell, where they will be "salted with fire." "Salt" in this instance was a shared word linking the ending of this passage to the following two sentences. Neither of these phrases has anything to do with the other or the one that precedes, except for the word "salt," which, it has been suggested, connected them orally and mnemonically. Mark apparently was reluctant to discard a tradition traced to Jesus but did not put much effort into making these verses congruous with each other.

gotten and, perhaps, that disagreements between eyewitnesses would surface. You might find that certain events are interpreted differently by the participants, depending on frame of reference, or that witnesses remember events in diverse sequences. As the frequent public disputes surrounding the biographies of famous people indicate, the creation of biographies can be quite contentious. As the chronicler, it would be your responsibility to settle such differences and to create an order for the material that would make it coherent and sensible for the reader. You might even have to be "creative" to make one event flow smoothly into the next, lest your narrative be jerky and abrupt, jumping from one event to another without meaningful, orderly connections. Among your most important considerations, shaping everything you wrote, would be the question of audience. The style and content of a biography that would appeal to the general public, and sell well in the popular market, would differ dramatically from that of an historical monograph intended for academia.

The production of the gospels was no less complex and contentious. As part of this process, there is evidence of intervening oral and literary collections of events from Jesus' life, his pithy sayings, parables he taught, miracles he worked, favorite teachings, and the like. Some vestiges of these collections seem to survive in the gospels.[7] As one might expect, by the time the evangelists were compiling the gospels many of these essential items from Jesus' life had become disconnected from their actual setting. There were also disputed and even outright spurious materials from existing second- and third-century writings.[8]

It fell to the four evangelists to gather these collections, winnowing the wheat from the chaff, the authentic material from the false, and form them into cohesive narrative accounts of the events and teachings of Jesus' public life. This development of the traditions around Jesus necessitated a certain amount of creativity on the part of the evangelists. They had to fashion the many different elements of the traditions as they were received, as isolated events and sayings or non-narrative collections, into interesting and informative accounts that would respond to the interests and pastoral needs of their individual intended audiences. To accomplish this, the composers needed to create some (most?) settings outright, crafting contexts for those teachings and events that had become detached from their original settings in the decades between Jesus' life and the composition of the gospels. Even where narratives had been remembered intact, their contexts

---

[7] For a parable collection see Mark 4:2-33.

[8] For colorful and disturbing images of the childhood of Jesus see *The Infancy Gospel of Thomas*.

may have been lost over time, requiring the production of narrative bridges that moved the action sensibly from one scene to the next.

For example, Luke knew that Jesus taught in parables, and he had received some parables that had been attributed to Jesus, among them the Parable of the Good Samaritan (Luke 10:30-35).[9] None of the other evangelists seems to have had this parable, or if they did, they chose not to include it. Luke also shared with Mark and Matthew a tradition wherein Jesus discusses the greatest commandments of the Law, that is, the love of God and one's neighbor (Mark 12:28-34//Matt 22:34-40). Both Mark's and Matthew's versions bring this legal discussion to a simple close. Luke, however, very creatively placed the parable, which presumably came to him detached from any original context, at the end of this discussion of the Law. To accomplish this in a way that flowed smoothly he had to reshape the ending of the discussion of the Law with the lawyer to create a bridge between it and the parable. Thus Luke has the scholar of the Law ask, as the other evangelists do not, "But who is my neighbor?" Jesus is then able to respond with the parable of the Good Samaritan. By choosing to place it here Luke has addressed an important issue for his largely non-Jewish audience, affirming that non-Jews were able to fulfill the most important summary elements of the Law. Very artfully, Luke has the lawyer ask the question most of us would ask, "Who is my neighbor?" but has Jesus redirect us to consider the more important question: "Whose neighbor will I be?"

Those who are most concerned about *history* might say, "But that is not how it really happened!" and they would most likely be correct. If our interest, however, is the person and teachings of Jesus we might better consider if this adaptation actually reflected who Jesus was, how he taught, and the content of his teaching. The question posed would not be "Was this a *fact?*" but "Could we consider this *true* to Jesus?" The early Christian communities that gathered the different gospels together, and chose from among them the four that expressed for them the faith they had received, were as capable as we are of perceiving the difference between Luke's version and those found in Mark and Matthew, and also between "fact" and "truth."

The process of gathering and accepting the various books into the canon of the New Testament took centuries of discussion and disagreement before a consensus was reached as to what belonged and what did not among the many things written in this period. The four gospels in the New Testament replicated, in written form, what the early Christian communities believed about the person of Jesus and the content of his teaching, and

---

[9] See also Luke 5:36; 6:39; 8:4; 12:16; 13:6; 14:7; 15:3; 18:1; 19:11; 20:9.

found trustworthy in light of the testimony they had received from eye-witness and other trusted sources (Luke 1:1-4). They were judged to be "true."

2. The Key to Redaction Criticism:
Links Between Matthew, Mark, and Luke

As becomes evident, the creation of the gospels was not a simple process, but one in which the gospel writers acted as editors of the material they received, shaping it into believable narratives they hoped would inter-est and spiritually edify their readers. Redaction criticism, a method for the critical study of the Bible, and the gospels in particular, studies the evange-lists' editorial process, that is, the way they adapted their many traditions, to discover how even the smallest modifications might reveal differences of nuance, theology, location, the cultures of the authors and the readers, the local conditions that prompted the composition of the gospel, and the like. It does so by analyzing what is distinctive to each gospel writer's perspective, examining among other items what the evangelists included and excluded, how they altered their shared traditions, how they organized their material, what themes they emphasized and repeated, and how they shaped transitions from one scene to the next.[10]

The foundation for redaction criticism is a widely accepted, though admittedly hypothetical, explanation of the historical development of three of the gospels. At the heart of it is the scholarly presupposition, unprovable yet still largely convincing, that both Matthew and Luke had separate ac-cess to the Gospel of Mark, which they used as a literary foundation for the composition of their own gospels, and to which they added additional materials.

It has long been noted that all the gospels overlap each other in some details, to greater and lesser degrees. While the Gospel of John is most distinctive, containing the largest quantity of unique material, Matthew,

---

[10] To be clear, although redaction criticism focuses on where subsequent writings are distinctive, it would be an error to consider only those areas where they are unique as truly representative of an author's thought. Everything an author uses, whether originating in one of her sources or created by her, has to be considered hers by virtue of its inclusion in her text. Whether Luke borrowed material, even word for word, from another source such as the Gospel of Mark, or created it outright, the presumption is that he did so because he thought it expressed his understanding of the person of Jesus, his behavior, or his teaching, and that it was useful for his own purpose of instructing his audience, since it reflected in an accurate and orderly manner "the matters that had been fulfilled and handed down" to him by those who "were eyewitnesses from the beginning and servants of the word" (Luke 1:1-3).

Mark, and Luke share quite a large amount of common material between them. In fact, roughly eighty-five percent of Mark, the shortest gospel, comprises fifty percent of Matthew's longer gospel, and roughly forty percent of Luke's gospel, the longest of the three. Much of this shared material was not only in the same order in the three gospels, but frequently used the same or similar vocabulary, often comprising the general outline of their narratives. What first drew people's attention to this similarity was the ease with which these three gospels could be viewed and compared together side by side, in columns. As a result, Matthew, Mark, and Luke have come to be known as the "synoptic gospels." "Synoptic" means "with the eye," referring to these readily visible similarities between them.

Since the process of sharing material by word of mouth inevitably leads to wide variation in content, diverse vocabulary, and large-scale rearrangement of material, the close correspondence between these three gospels indicates that, at least in regard to their shared material, they were composed from a common written source. Their similarity necessitated some linking document shared by all three gospel writers. The easiest, most efficient solution would be that one of the gospels served as a foundation for the other two. Two theories have been proposed along this line, one suggesting that Matthew was the original, the other Mark. Although both have reasons for and against them, the latter suggestion, that Mark was the first written, has become the overwhelming favorite in the scholarly community.

Mark has 660 verses, of which roughly 600 are incorporated into Matthew and approximately 560 into Luke.[11] Of this shared material, almost all of it is in the same order in all three texts. Occasionally either Matthew or Luke will vary the order as found in Mark, but they never reorder their texts in identical fashion. In those instances in which Luke differs from Mark's order, Matthew always agrees with Mark. In the same way, wherever Matthew varies from Mark's arrangement, Luke always sides with Mark. Again, it never happens that Matthew and Luke have a common order deviating from Mark.

Furthermore, since Matthew contains fifty percent more material than Mark, and Luke sixty percent more, if one was to suggest that either of them was first it would be difficult to explain why Mark would have suppressed their additional material. Although some few have suggested, in fact, that Mark is an "abridged" version of Matthew, there have been few

---

[11] More precise numbers cannot be given since each of the gospels is numbered differently, and not all shared materials coincide exactly with verse divisions.

convincing explanations of Mark's motivation for deleting important material, such as the Sermon on the Mount from Matthew or some of Luke's beautiful and moving parables. Another problem would be accounting for Mark's decision to "tarnish" his source, substituting his own coarser and more awkward expressions for Matthew's or Luke's generally superior Greek grammar and vocabulary. Indeed, it would be much easier to accept that Matthew and Luke had corrected Mark than the reverse.[12]

Admittedly, there are some problems with the theory of Markan priority. For example, Luke omitted a sizable portion of material (Mark 6:45–8:26), leaving us to explain why Luke, if he had a complete copy of Mark's gospel, would delete so much information. This section contains a varied series of stories, including repeated mentions of the hardness of the disciples' hearts and their incapacity to understand Jesus' identity (Mark 6:45-52; 8:11-21), the curing of multitudes of sick (Mark 6:53-56) and of a deaf man (Mark 7:31-37), a controversy between Jesus and the Pharisees about the washing of hands (Mark 7:1-23), an episode in which Jesus refers to a Syrophoenician woman as a dog but then cures her daughter (Mark 7:24-30), a repeat of the "multiplication of the loaves" (Mark 8:1-10), and the double cure of the blind man (Mark 8:22-26).

It is possible that Luke's version of Mark may have been incomplete, partial, or damaged, omitting the missing Markan content. It seems more likely, however, that Luke's overall length was the deciding factor in the omission. It is readily noted that both the Gospel of Luke and the Acts of the Apostles are roughly the same size and would have been on the longer side, amply filling a conventional scroll. Though technically scrolls can be made of any size, after a certain point they were unwieldy for the reader. Luke and Acts are just at the breaking point of "user friendliness." It is suggested that Luke had so much additional material to add to what he received from Mark that he had to choose between his received traditions to fit them onto one reasonably large scroll. In the end he deleted repeated stories (e.g., the multiplication of the loaves), miracles that bordered on the superstitious or the magical (the use of spittle to effect cures, or the touching of talismans, i.e., Jesus' clothes), material about Jewish cultic rituals that did not apply to Luke's target Gentile readers (the hand-washing controversy), and stories offensive to Luke's intended audience (the cure of the Gentile Syrophoenician's daughter).

Another difficulty for those proposing Markan priority are the instances of minor agreements, shared by Matthew and Luke over against

---

[12] Joseph A. Fitzmyer, *The Gospel According to Luke I–IX* (New York: Doubleday, 1979) 686.

what they received from Mark. For example, when, after John the Baptist's execution, Jesus withdrew with his disciples to an uninhabited place (Mark 6:31-32), the people noted it and hurried on ahead of them. Both Matthew 14:13 and Luke 9:11 altered Mark's text in similar fashion, saying that when the crowds "heard" (Matthew) or "knew" (Luke), they *followed,* rather than preceding him. This kind of similarity is harder to explain, since scholars are reluctant to suggest too many coincidences. It is possible that in these instances Matthew and Luke both had yet *another* non-Markan, yet still written version of this story that they both coincidentally preferred over Mark's. The necessity of supplying additional shared written sources is admittedly awkward, but possible.

Both Matthew and Luke also make similar deletions and emendations of their Markan original. Some of the deletions are easily explained by the negative or emotional portrayal of Jesus in Mark, which both Matthew and Luke seem to have found objectionable. For example, it is easy to see why both might independently delete the account in which Jesus' relatives set out to seize him because they have concluded that he is mad (Mark 3:20-21), or the awkward moment when Jesus is unable to cure the blind man on the first try (Mark 8:22-26).

Although there are some real difficulties for the hypothesis of Markan priority, the overwhelming majority of scholars prefer it due to the even greater problems attached to the less-popular theory of Matthean priority. Once accepted, though, this theory leaves open a rich opportunity for studying both Matthew and Luke in light of the changes they make to their Markan original. For example, certain trends are discerned, such as Matthew's consistent interest in explaining Jesus' relationship with Torah, that demonstrate a greater understanding of and interest in Jewish practices and belief. This suggests that Matthew, and a large part of his intended audience, may have been converts to Christianity from Judaism. Luke's alterations of his Markan source also reveal much about him and his community, as we will see below.

3. *Mark, "Q," and the Multiple Source Theory*

There is also a body of material shared by Matthew and Luke that is not found in Mark, largely composed of sayings and parables of Jesus. It amounts to about twenty-four passages, or between 220 and 235 verses. Only three passages in this material are narrative in character, including the three temptations of Jesus (Luke 4:3-13//Matt 4:3-11), the centurion's sick servant (Luke 7:2-10//Matt 8:5-13), and the address to Jesus by the disciples of John the Baptist (Luke 7:18-23//Matt 11:2-6). Thirteen of these twenty-four passages are found in the same order in both gospels. Again the language between the two versions is not identical, but so similar that scholars have to assume the existence of a written document, available and used by both Luke and Matthew. This document has come to be known as "Q," the initial for the German word *Quelle,* meaning "source." "Q's" existence remains purely speculative, since there is no extant copy of this text.

Thus it can be said that the gospels of Luke and Matthew share two major sources for their content, the Gospel of Mark and "Q." Luke also has some unique content found only in his gospel, commonly referred to as "L," as does Matthew, material known as "M." For our purposes it is unnecessary to determine whether "L" or "M" came to their respective evangelists orally or in written form, in large collections or as many distinct traditions. There are two names used to describe this solution to explain the similarities between Matthew, Mark, and Luke. The first, the "two-source hypothesis," reflects the two shared sources, Mark and "Q." The second and ever more common description, since it more accurately acknowledges the existence of both "L" and "M," is the "multiple source hypothesis."

Once it had been determined likely that Matthew and Luke had made use of these sources, it was also noticed that they each had distinctive ways of utilizing their shared resources. For example, they shared the tendency to soften Mark's presentation of the disciples as obtuse. In Luke's case we find that he occasionally rearranged the material he received from Mark for the sake of consecutiveness, inserting material to prepare for later developments and providing a literary pattern of prophecy and fulfillment. He apparently found some of Mark's vocabulary vulgar, inaccurate, or perhaps offensive, since he upgraded Mark's diction, grammar, and syntax. Mark was not overly concerned with consistency in tenses or agreement in gender, syntactical case, and number between antecedents of pronouns and adjectives or subjects and verbs. This evidenced a lack of refinement Luke did not share and would not replicate. Mark's text was also sometimes confusing, so, where necessary, Luke clarified his Markan material. We presume that if he found it necessary to modify Mark he may also have felt obliged and empowered to edit and refine his other sources as well. Although such grammatical and syntactical corrections are usually not indicative of distinctive theologies, they are an indication of Luke's probable social location among the classically educated. In the case of Luke's relationship with Mark we have an extant text (Mark's) with which to make comparisons. We have no extant text of "Q." Thus redaction studies of Luke's and Matthew's use of "Q" are more difficult, though not impossible. Once patterns of correction and alteration of Mark are determined for either Matthew or Luke we can extrapolate that each would have followed similar patterns in their alterations of "Q."

A final but important point about the aims of redaction criticism: It would be possible to use the process of redaction criticism to unpeel the editorial additions and alterations to early traditions with the aim of reconstructing the original event in the life of Jesus, unvarnished by subsequent accretions. Such a purpose, however, while not at all antithetical to the proper ends of redaction criticism, is not essential to them, either. The most deliberate level of focus is not on recovering Jesus' historical moment, or even, necessarily, on understanding how the other participants in the events of his life would have interpreted them. Redaction criticism more properly focuses on that later editorial and authorial office of the evangelists, in the case of the gospels, and their purposes in shaping those same events into a narrative in the way they do for the audience they had.

Luke's Editorial Style

It will aid our study of Luke's version of the anointing story if we begin with a working knowledge of how Luke typically interacted editorially, by way of style and methodology, with the rest of his Markan material. Again, some 560 verses of Mark's 660, or roughly forty percent of Luke's content, originated in Mark, and *usually* in the same sequence. While we cannot carefully study every change instituted by Luke, it would be helpful to understand the general trends that become evident through a close comparison of the Lukan and Markan texts. To state the conclusion in advance, what we find is that Luke was a careful and consistent, but not rash, editor of Mark's gospel, largely respecting Mark's order and content. It will be important to keep this in mind when the focus is primarily on Luke's modifications.

We can deduce from his gospel's opening verses that his intention in composing a new gospel was more than simply to add his unique material to the works of the many who had attempted "to arrange a narrative" (1:1). From the beginning he desired to set out the traditions anew, implying that those such as Mark and "Q" who had already done so had failed to provide an orderly arrangement (Luke 1:1-4). His own intent was to do it "accurately," and thus to correct, as we shall see, whatever, either by arrangement or content, appeared erroneous, unreasonable, confusing, or inapplicable to his audience. As in the case of the great omission of Mark 6:45–8:26, his most marked infidelity to Mark as already discussed above, when Luke chose not to follow Mark his motivations are often immediately apparent or become so after the consistent patterns of emendation are recognized.

Luke, as any good author would, edited his sources to suit them to his Greek audience. Where in Mark the paralytic's attendants open up the Palestinian earth and straw roof to let down the paralytic (Mark 2:4), Luke accommodates the story to his audience's own Hellenistic, tile-roofed architecture (Luke 5:19). Where Mark's Jesus spoke of "great ones" who have authority over others (Mark 10:42), Luke's Jesus, in proper upper-crust Hellenistic fashion, referred to these great ones as "benefactors" (Luke 22:25).

It did happen, in fact, that Luke discovered errors of fact in the Gospel of Mark. For example, Luke omitted Mark's mistaken reference to David's encounter with the high priest Abiathar in Mark 2:26 since, in fact, Ahimelech was high priest at the time.[13] Again, where Mark imprecisely refers to "King Herod" (Mark 6:14), Luke provides the more exact title of "Herod the tetrarch," meaning "subordinate ruler" (Luke 9:7).

Luke displays a clear aversion for the unreasonable. For instance, Simon, Andrew, James, and John leave behind everything, including their livelihoods, to follow Jesus at what would appear to be their first encounter of him, with no apparent indication in Mark's text that they have ever seen Jesus in action or heard his teaching. Luke makes two changes in his sequence of narrative events to provide them a rational motivation for their radical decision. In the first place Luke moves the cure of Simon's mother-in-law, which in Mark follows the call of the disciples, to a new place in his gospel, before the summons. Then, he inserts a new story immediately before the call, in which Jesus wondrously helps Simon Peter capture a large catch of fish.[14] With these shifts Luke enabled the four men, having witnessed these wonders, to make an informed decision to abandon their livelihoods and accept Jesus' invitation to become his disciples.

Luke makes several such "reasonable improvements" to his Markan original, often for the sake of clarity. In the episode in which Jesus is asked to cure a man's child, Mark's Jesus confusingly appears to require Jairus, the father of the dead daughter, to remain outside his own house, only to place him inside somewhat later (Mark 5:37, 40). Luke, on the other hand, provides a more consistent narrative in which it is clear that Jairus has accompanied Jesus into his house from the beginning (Luke 8:51). Where Mark has a blind man jump up and approach Jesus (Mark 10:50), Luke, more sensibly, has the man brought to him (Luke 18:40). When Mark's

---

[13] Luke 6:4; see 1 Sam 21:2-7.

[14] The Markan order: the call of the disciples (Mark 1:16-18); the cure of Simon Peter's mother-in-law (Mark 1:30-31). The Lukan order: the cure of Simon Peter's mother-in-law (Luke 4:38); the great catch of fish (Luke 5:1-9); the call of the disciples (Luke 5:9-11).

crowds are amazed at seeing Jesus for no apparent cause, Luke omits their astonishment.[15] Where Jesus gives a troublingly disjointed teaching on salt (Mark 9:49-50), Luke keeps the core of the tradition but discards the rest (Luke 14:34-35). Luke slightly emends Mark's version of the parable of the vineyard so that it more closely resembles Jesus' execution outside the city of Jerusalem (Mark 12:8//Luke 20:15) and then, in case the reader should miss the point, adds the clarification that the parable was aimed at the scribes and chief priests (Luke 20:19).

Further Lukan changes were stylistic in nature. For example, Luke was dissatisfied with Mark's "chatty" style and consistently condensed Mark's stories, reducing verbosity in general and removing lengthy explanations, especially material that was of greater interest to Jews than to Gentiles.[16] For example, in Mark, Jesus and the Pharisees discuss Moses' acquiescence to effortless divorce; Jesus then quotes Scripture to ground his rejection of this current Jewish practice; the disciples inquire about Jesus' position in private; finally Jesus offers a pronouncement, forbidding remarriage after divorce (Mark 10:2-12). Luke deletes over one hundred words in Greek from this episode, removing everything except the essential detail of Jesus' final pronouncement on divorce (Luke 16:18).

One of Mark's consistent patterns was to include the Hebrew and Aramaic terms and phrases that accompanied his sources, such as *talitha koum* (Mark 5:41), usually providing a translation, in this case "little girl, [I tell you] get up," for his Greek-speaking audience.[17] Luke, or perhaps his audience, was apparently sufficiently removed from any interest in such things that he found it preferable to remove almost all the Aramaic terminology, leaving only *pascha,* or "Passover," for which Luke provides the questionable translation of "Feast of Unleavened Bread."[18]

Mark enthusiastically emphasized important themes and events by repeating them. Luke's inclination, perhaps for simple lack of space, was to eliminate the repetitious material. So where Mark included two multiplications of the loaves, Luke retained only one.[19] While Jesus cured two

---

[15] Mark 9:15//Luke 9:38; Mark 10:32//Luke 18:31.

[16] Mark 10:2-12//Luke 16:18; Mark 11:15-17//Luke 19:45-46; Mark 1:41-42//Luke 5:13; Mark 5:2-5//Luke 8:27, 29; Mark 10:23-24//Luke 18:24; Mark 11:15-17//Luke 19:45-46.

[17] See also *Boanerges,* 3:17; *qorban,* 7:11; *ephphatha,* 7:34; *Bartimaeus,* 10:46; *hosanna,* 11:9-10; *pascha,* 14:1; *abba,* 14:36; *rabbi,* 14:45; *Golgotha,* 15:22; *Eloi, Eloi, lema sabachthani?* 15:34.

[18] Lev 23:5-6 demonstrates that these two feasts, though adjacent in the Jewish calendar, are not identical.

[19] Mark 6:32-44; 8:1-10//Luke 9:10-17.

blind men in Mark, there is only one fully recounted narrative of a like cure in Luke, though he acknowledged Jesus had cured many of their blindness.[20] All this served to tighten up Luke's account.

As any text reveals something about the capacity of its author, we can consider whether Luke's preference for portraying Jesus and the disciples behaving in a readily perceptible lucid manner says as much about them as it does about Luke, his character, personality, audience, and social setting.[21] In this regard it is useful to keep the preceding evidence in mind when considering Luke's most typical comprehensive modifications, which were to upgrade the prose of the narrative, mending Mark's fractured syntax and enhancing his vocabulary throughout his own edition of the gospel. Since modern biblical translators and editors are *also* inclined to fix these kinds of blemishes, they are all but invisible in modern translations and would require overly technical explanations to demonstrate. These kinds of modifications, especially when taken in light of Luke's inclination to repair Mark's wordiness and lack of clarity, suggest not simply intelligence, a quality amply displayed by the author of Mark as well, but a sophistication to be found usually among the well educated. Returning to historical and cultural considerations, we note that only a small percentage of people in the ancient world had access to that kind of education, and they tended to be the affluent landed elite.

Some of Luke's editing was more than stylistic, however, for he was apparently unhappy with the theological message of some Markan content. As an example, Luke alters Mark's description of the Spirit *driving* Jesus *out* into the desert (Mark 1:12) into a more congenial portrayal of Jesus being *led* by the Spirit into the desert (Luke 4:1). Luke in fact places a greater emphasis on the Holy Spirit, with sixteen mentions in comparison to Mark's six.[22]

Another area of particular dissatisfaction for Luke was Mark's unflattering portrayal of Jesus' disciples, either individually, as in the case of Peter, or as a group. Luke had a different, more positive sense of them, and made both subtle and overt changes to represent them favorably. For example, where Peter appears critical of Jesus' withdrawal from his healing ministry in Mark (Mark 1:36), Luke deletes the comment, and instead portrays the crowd as importunate (Luke 4:42). He likewise eliminates both

---

[20] Mark 8:22-26; 10:46-52//Luke 7:21; 18:35-43.

[21] For examples of such, compare the following: Mark 14:1//Luke 22:1; Mark 14:11//Luke 22:6; Mark 15:1-2//Luke 23:1-3.

[22] Mark 1:8, 10, 12; 3:29; 12:36; 13:11; Luke 1:15, 35, 41, 67; 2:25, 26, 27; 3:16, 22; 4:1, 14, 18; 10:21; 11:13; 12:10, 12.

Peter's rejection of the Messiah's suffering and Jesus' harsh rebuke in response (Mark 8:32//Luke 9:23), and softens Jesus' rebuke of the sleeping Peter (Mark 14:37//Luke 22:45-46). In Luke, Peter does not contest Jesus' prediction of his denial, as he does in Mark (Mark 14:30-31//Luke 22:34). Finally, Luke balances Peter's betrayal by inserting Jesus' acknowledgment that Peter will recover and serve as a source of strength for others (Luke 22:31-32).

In regard to the disciples as a group, Mark's Jesus asks them how it is that they have no faith (Mark 4:40) or understanding (4:13), while Luke's Jesus wants to know *where* their faith is (Luke 8:25) and pays no heed to their lack of understanding (8:9-10). While in Mark the disciples are too obtuse to understand Jesus' teaching (Mark 9:32), in Luke the meaning was hidden from them so that, for the time being, they could not understand (Luke 9:45).[23] As for the disciples' behavior, although they will still dispute who should be the greatest, James and John will not make their audacious request to sit at Jesus' right and left in the kingdom, as they do in Mark.[24]

Luke also redeems Jesus' family from Mark's relentlessly unflattering portrayal. Jesus' kin come to seize him in Mark 3:21, claiming that he is "beside himself." Luke, of course, deletes this passage altogether. Again in Mark, Jesus' mother and brothers arrive and summon Jesus while he is engaged in teaching. He responds by distinguishing his family outside from his *real* mother and brothers, that is, those sitting around him and doing the Father's will (Mark 3:31-34). In Luke 8:19-20, when his family are unable to join him, rather than sending for him they request to see him. Luke's Jesus then includes all who hear and act on the word of God, even his blood relatives, in a familial relationship. Luke sets this up carefully, having already skillfully portrayed Jesus' mother, Mary, as the first in the gospel to model appropriate implementation of God's will.[25]

As in the case of the disciples and the family, Luke also consistently altered unflattering elements of Mark's depictions of Jesus. For example, Mark shows characters directly disobeying Jesus' commands. Luke was uncomfortable with displays of insubordination.[26] Mark was seemingly comfortable with chaotic human dynamics, since he recounts how Jesus almost loses control of the crowd around him while curing the sick (Mark 3:9-10). Luke, by quietly deleting this detail, allows Jesus to maintain an

---

[23] Compare also Mark 6:52; 8:17, 21 and Luke 18:34; 24:45.

[24] Mark 10:35-41//Luke 22:24.

[25] Luke 8:21; see also 1:35-38.

[26] Contrast Mark 1:44-45 and Luke 5:14-15.

aura of authority and power in the same situation (Luke 6:19). Again, while Jesus' exorcisms in Mark's gospel can be dramatic, if somewhat messy, as in the continuing struggle of the mute and deaf spirit as it is exorcized (Mark 9:26), Jesus' control over such spirits in Luke's gospel is instantaneously effective (Luke 9:42). Mark even reported that Jesus was *not able* to work any miracles in Nazareth (Mark 6:1-6). Luke, however, clarifies that, like the great prophets before him, he was *not sent* to perform such there (Luke 4:16-30). These alterations manifest Jesus' power and reinforce his authority.

Luke also frequently eliminates implications of ignorance implied by Jesus' inquiries. In Mark 9:21-24 Jesus compassionately asks the father of the apparently epileptic boy how long his son has suffered from seizures. In Luke 9:42 Jesus moves directly to the cure without the investigation. Where Mark's Jesus will ask the disciples what they were arguing about (Mark 9:33), Luke's Jesus already knows not only the content of their argument, but also the disposition of their hearts (Luke 9:47).

Luke, it would seem, preferred to portray Jesus as a Hellenistic gentleman, temperate and self-controlled. Mark's Jesus could suggest, with dramatic and certainly hyperbolic enthusiasm, the amputation of offending limbs and eyes lest the whole person perish (Mark 9:43). Luke fails to include this passage. While it is probably too bold to claim that Luke was a Stoic, he reveals that, like many of his contemporaries in the first-century Hellenistic world, he had been influenced by some Stoic values. In that spirit Luke tends to delete frequent Markan references to Jesus' strong emotions such as anger, indignation, and even love,[27] or public displays of affection.[28] An exception to this is Luke's addition that Jesus wept over Jerusalem, where he includes a description of how, by Luke's own time, the Romans had indeed surrounded and destroyed the city (Luke 19:41-44).[29]

The difference between the two Passion stories is a revealing study of contrasts. In Mark, Jesus is distraught and sorrowing, a pawn of the Father's will, falling to the ground in his anguish (Mark 14:33-36), and dramatically abandoned by his disciples (Mark 14:50-52). In Luke, having advised his companions to pray, Jesus calmly kneels to do the same (Luke 22:40-42). In Mark, Jesus is never exonerated. In Luke, Pilate repeatedly announces a judgment of innocence (Luke 23:4, 14-15, 22). In Mark, Jesus'

[27] Mark 3:5//Luke 6:10; Mark 10:14//Luke 18:16; Mark 10:21//Luke 18:22.
[28] Mark 9:36//Luke 9:47; Mark 10:15-16//Luke 18:17.
[29] Note that Luke 22:43-44, the episode in which Jesus weeps blood, is almost certainly an ancient addition to Luke's gospel.

only response to the torture and taunting is his last impassioned words quoting the opening verse of Psalm 22, "My God, my God, why have you abandoned me?" The sense of loss, pain, and alienation are palpable. This is far too bleak and disturbing for Luke, whose Jesus goes to his destiny calmly, instructing the women of Jerusalem (23:27-31), offering hope to doomed criminals (23:39-43), accompanied by heavenly portents (23:44-45), and surrendering his spirit with high drama and dignified self-control (23:46). Jesus' last words are appropriately assuring and self-possessed: "Into your hands I entrust my spirit" (Ps 31:6). Nothing happens to Luke's Jesus, including the passing of his life, except that Jesus first wills it.

Such alterations demonstrate that there are distinctive elements of Luke's theology when compared to Mark's regarding the person of Jesus, the significance of his death, the nature of discipleship, and the relationship between the Savior and the Spirit. For those who base their faith on a literal or overly historicized reading of these Scriptures such variations may be troubling. The contemporary pursuit of the *one* correct way to express faith is apparently more static and monochromatic than the faith life expressed in the gospels of the early church. Appreciation of the variation in the early church, providing breadth and depth for contemporary models of theological discussion, may free us to accept multiple expressions of faith in God now.

Having emphasized, however, what is distinctive in Luke, we should point out again that there is even more similarity than divergence. We are able to recognize the Jesus of Mark in the Jesus of Luke. This brings us to the question of how Luke resolves alterations of his other sources. In the absence of an existing text we cannot say with certainty the extent of what Luke received from "L," but when faced with the choice between Luke as a radical revisionist, as opposed to a sympathetic and gentle emendator, the latter seems more consistent with Luke's approach. As we shall see, this is an important question for the resolution of Luke 7:36-50, since Luke drew on both Mark and "L" in its composition.

CHAPTER TWO

Culture, First-Century Judaism, and Christianity

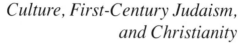

Methodology: Anthropology

In essence anthropology, like literary criticism, is hermeneutical, since the fundamental issue of anthropology is interpretation.[1] In its proper role it studies unfamiliar cultures and seeks, while not sacrificing what is authentically different, to make the foreign understandable, though not necessarily familiar. In fact, it sometimes is drawn to what is different and distinctive.

It is precisely for this reason that the protocols and insights of anthropology are useful for the study of biblical texts. Though these texts have become familiar to some today, through liturgy and study, they remain products of ancient and still *unfamiliar* cultures. In point of fact, whenever we read the Bible we are participating in cross-cultural communication. To that extent, while it may be possible to determine what any given text means to the reader, it is a more challenging task to determine what the text meant to those who produced or first read it.

Both humans and their cultures, while not precisely intangible, lest there be nothing to study, are fluid, ever changing in sometimes unpredictable fashion. So, by virtue of its studied ends, anthropology is unable to replicate its findings in strictly controlled environments with determined variables and is not properly a hard science, although some would like to treat it in this fashion.

---

[1] Clifford Geertz, *The Interpretation of Cultures: Selected Essays* (New York: Basic Books, 1973) 1–5.

Non-analytical Anthropology: There are various approaches to the question of anthropology's proper ends. The simplest of these would be a non-analytical approach, that is, the recording of observations of the studied culture, collecting isolated historical or social facts as data with no more analysis than necessary to explain it in intelligible terms and lacking in any comparisons of the behavior of the studied culture to the practices of any other. This approach can be interesting, if one is curious and the studied culture is different enough from one's culture of origin, but is not helpful when approaching a people with the desire for understanding. The recording of similar and dissimilar cultural practices is not particularly useful if you do not understand *why* the different cultures do what they do, which is only possible in contextual studies. For this reason, this approach was largely abandoned by anthropologists.

It would be particularly unsatisfactory as a basis for interpreting what we find in the Scriptures. For the sake of understanding, we need to do more to inform ourselves of the *interrelations* of texts, social contexts, concepts, familial and communal behavior, status, belief systems, and ideologies in order to construct the prerequisite cultural picture that will enable the other biblical criticisms to accomplish their ends in an informed manner, understanding what authors said and intended within the boundaries of *their own* environment.[2] As for the socio-scientific biblical methods, anthropology has often been used in the background, providing better understandings of the cultures that produced biblical texts and influencing, in often subliminal fashion, the informed reader's interpretation of the text.

Comparative Anthropology: The comparative (or nomothetic) approach to anthropology's starting premise is that there is a common, foundational humanity underlying all cultures that, if observed carefully, can provide generalizing propositions and categories that could be understood as normative for all human cultures, independent of time or place.[3] Such an anthropology seeks to answer the large questions of human behavior by comparing the similarities and disparities of cultures. This approach comes closest to using a scientific approach to culture, seeking through testing and observation to determine how environmental conditions determine human behaviors according to recognizable patterns.

---

[2] John H. Elliott, *What is Social-Scientific Criticism?* (Philadelphia: Fortress, 1993) 13–14.

[3] See A.R. Radcliffe-Brown, "The Comparative Method in Social Anthropology," in Adam Kuper, ed., *The Social Anthropology of Radcliffe-Brown* (London: Routledge & Kegan Paul, 1977) 53–69.

Unfortunately, and as a critique of the comparative approach, in the study of human cultures exceptions to general principles have been the norm. Individuals and cultures do not seem to respond to identical stimuli in predictable patterns, and it only takes one contrary example to disprove a general principle. It has also been amply demonstrated that when comparisons are drawn between societal behaviors that have been divorced from their larger cultural contexts, the conclusions are often misleading. The attentive study of behaviors in context has led to further collapse of this approach since it is often the case that behaviors shared by different cultures do not always spring from like environmental or historical causes, leading to many dead ends in the pursuit of underlying principles of human behavior.[4]

There are anthropologists who continue to engage in comparative anthropology, in spite of its difficulties and failures. Again, this group is the most dedicated to anthropological study as a science.

Contextual Anthropology: The third anthropological approach, remaining in the scientific comparative fold to some extent, holds that cultures can only be understood within their own specific contexts, on their own terms, with particular focus on the meanings of beliefs and practices as understood by the participants within the culture. At first glance this would seem to be a move away from the comparative approach altogether. "Contextualists," as participants in this approach are sometimes called, have often been diffusionists, however, accepting that neighboring cultures interact and influence each other, and are therefore, although in a moderated fashion, still comparativists, simply on a smaller scale. For their part, even strict contextualists run into problems, often disagreeing on how broad a context is necessary to provide sufficient and accurate background information to build an accurate analysis of the studied cultures.[5]

This approach has been adopted, with mixed results, by several biblical scholars. Their work is noted for proposing general principles to describe the normative regional behavior of the peoples of the Mediterranean basin and extrapolating acceptable insider behavior and contrasting it with offensive outsider activities according to "boundaries" and categories of honor and shame.

The ultimate critique of the last two methods lies in their failure to produce the general principles they seek to find. Except for the broadest generalities about humans, such as that they find shelter from the elements,

---

[4]Franz Boas, "The Limitations of the Comparative Method," in idem, *Race, Language and Culture* (New York: Macmillan, 1940 [1896]) 273–75.

[5]Jerry D. Moore, *Visions of Culture* (Walnut Creek, CA: Alta Mira Press, 1997) 65.

they obtain food, and they procreate and nurture their young, the hunt for deeper patterns and substantial propositions has proved largely unsuccessful.[6]

Postmodern Anthropology: Contemporary anthropologists, exhausted by the failed search for general principles and underlying causes, and weary of determining the appropriate limits of context, often choose to focus on the *distinctiveness* of each culture. Proponents of this approach have produced a steadily growing chorus of criticism against the presumption of the scientific, comparative method. They claim (1) that the scientific comparative effort has often been ethnocentric and pro-western; (2) that it presumed relationships between divergent cultures that could not be verified by objective clinical testing; (3) that there was a need for a greater voice for the cultures being studied, claiming that "polyvocality" was restrained and orchestrated in traditional ethnographies, relegating the members of studied societies to the roles of sources, or "informants," to be quoted or paraphrased;[7] and (4) that the scientific premise of comparative work is utterly compromised by the need to hear from these other voices, other authorities, in an intersubjective dialogue that by its very nature qualifies the scientific project.[8]

They assert the appropriateness of studying each culture for its own sake, in all its uniqueness. They warn, though, that meanings attached to objects and behaviors by outside observers are arbitrary and dependent on the experiences the observers bring to the moment of evaluation and, as a result, are discountable. As a result they posit that insiders alone are effectively equipped to interpret the local meanings of the things they use and the actions they do.[9] Only after the studied community is given an ample opportunity to express *itself* to a discerning observer can understanding of a culture be achieved.

Anthropology and Biblical Studies

Whether anthropology's pursuit of broad, positively stated principles to clarify the traits of human cultures will ever prove fruitful is uncertain. It

---

[6]Geertz, *Interpretation of Cultures,* 34–43.

[7]James Clifford, "Partial Truths," in idem and George E. Marcus, eds., *Writing Culture: The Poetics and Politics of Ethnography* (Berkeley: University of California Press, 1986) 15.

[8]James Clifford, "On Ethnographic Allegory," in *Writing Culture,* 109.

[9]Keith H. Basso, "'Speaking with Names': Language and Landscape Among the Western Apache," in George E. Marcus, ed., *Rereading Cultural Anthropology* (Durham, NC: Duke University Press, 1992) 220.

may be too soon to discard the search completely, but the continued effort to produce general rules of human behavior does not properly belong to biblical scholarship and certainly ought not yet be presumed successful by those involved in it. Anthropologists may yet achieve that "critical mass" of information necessary to formulate principles, or again, they may not.

There does still remain, however, a whole realm of procedural insights from anthropology that are not without merit in themselves. The following observations are offered with the hope of prompting the development of an *anthropological consciousness* in those who engage seriously in biblical scholarship. This consciousness enables students of Scripture to avoid pitfalls and obtain as much insight as possible. It also sensitizes us to recognize evidence where it exists. The genius of the famous character of Sherlock Holmes was that he recognized what was truly significant. The hope is that an anthropological consciousness can enable readers of Scripture to ask the right questions of the texts they study, and to thereby uncover the motivations and perspectives of those who produced them.

Admitting the Difficulties: There are great difficulties for anyone seeking to use a cultural approach to the interpretation of the Bible. Even in the best of circumstances anthropologists are inclined to admit the many hurdles in the way of accurate interpretations of contemporary foreign cultures. This is all the more true for biblical scholarship, since it is the nature of the anthropological task, where possible, to live among, observe, interact with, and question the participants of the studied culture.[10] Unfortunately, the temporal distance between the first century and the twenty-first makes this impossible.

We have only the voices present in texts, corroborated or contradicted by archaeologists and historians. The evidence available simply does not answer all the questions we might ask of a living source. The consequence is that some questions will have no answers, some will only be answered hypothetically, and that contradictory data may leave us without the clarity we seek.

It is not altogether hopeless, though. The cooperation of archaeologists, Scripture scholars, historians, and the like, when perceived through an anthropological lens, do provide a certain amount of the "thick description" referred to by ethnographers. The more information we assemble, the better we will comprehend the pertinent cultures, integrating cultic systems within the broader cultural aspects of mating, agriculture, commerce,

---

[10]Victor Matthews and Don C. Benjamin, "Introduction: Social Sciences and Biblical Studies," *Semeia* 68 (1994) 12.

religion, etc., current at the time in Israelite, Jewish, and Hellenistic cultures, as distinct wholes, and as interrelated communities.[11]

Fortunately, other writings relatively contemporaneous to the New Testament, such as those by Josephus, Philo, and other extra-canonical witnesses, enable us to build an ever more helpful picture of the first-century cultures that produced the New Testament. The discovery of materials at Qumran, in particular, has widened the scope of observation considerably, and given modern scholars a much more informed view of one small portion of the political, religious, and social world of first-century Judaism.

Having admitted the difficulties involved, we next consider some procedural items.

Ethnocentrism: First, it is more helpful to the anthropological process to *report* than to *evaluate,* particularly if that means placing judgments. While it may be natural for ethnographers to consider their own way of life as rational and "civilized," while appraising others variously as intriguing, curious, quaint or, perhaps, unreasonable, they are encouraged to consciously set aside any ethnocentric or pro-Western bias.

For example, when doing biblical research Christians may conclude that they themselves are true and faithful, "worshiping the Father in spirit and truth" (John 4:23-24). Anthropologically, though, any tendency to prefer the familiar, such as those practices of the early church most closely resembling twenty-first-century Christian customs, while disparaging those most different, such as first-century Jewish Temple animal sacrifices, will interfere with our ability to understand with any objectivity.

The price paid for ethnocentric subjectivity will be a tendency to color, even distort, portrayals of Second Temple Judaism and early Christianity. It has led to unduly negative portrayal of Jews, particularly as early Christians negotiated their own sense of loss at the destruction of the Temple and their exclusion from the synagogue. A sensitive reading of the text, unencumbered by a preference for the familiar, helps us appreciate, for example, the struggles of a significant portion of the early church, drawn from Judaism or sympathetic to its beliefs, values, and practices, that felt an urgency to maintain some or all of the customs of their past life. If we fail to acknowledge their sense of alienation and loss, resulting from

---

[11]By "thick description" I refer, in essence, to that critical mass of information desirable for understanding the complexities that underlie a given culture's behavior. It necessarily includes descriptions of as many aspects of the studied culture as possible, including beliefs, cult, mating rituals, economy, dietary practices, child rearing, etc. It is based on the premise that these differing aspects of cultural life are all interrelated (see Geertz, *Interpretation of Cultures*).

how *positively* they evaluated their Jewish way of life, we can hardly hope to understand the struggles in the Galatian community, or Paul's pastoral motivations or rhetorical strategies in his letter to the Romans. This anthropological advice should make sense to those who prefer exegetical reading strategies, drawing meaning out of texts, to eisegetical readings that impose meanings on them.

Metaphoric Interpretation: Conversely, it is understandable that, in the effort to make sense out of cultures different from our own, we compare elements of the studied culture to aspects of the more familiar world from which we come. Ethnographers, however, are discouraged from drawing any unnecessary correlations between the studied culture and their own, even where the similarities *appear* to be strong. Such comparisons inevitably obscure as much as, if not more than, they clarify.

For example, the gospels refer to "lawyers," or "scholars of the law" (Matt 25:35; Luke 7:30), a profession that exists in our day. Sometimes their roles and responsibilities overlap, and sometimes they do *not*. American humor often pokes fun at the legal profession, even unfairly so, for being shark-like and avaricious. To make presumptions about the education, attitudes, or lifestyles of such professions based on modern equivalents easily leads to misunderstanding. Overlaying a modern perception of lawyers on those depicted in the gospels dulls the reader's perception to the probability that most lawyers in Jesus' day were highly respected, not for their wealth or fierce litigiousness, but for their capacity to recollect and interpret God's law. This makes Jesus' judgments of the lawyers in Luke 11:45-52 all the more shocking.

Another example is that of slavery. The American experience of reducing an entire race of people to slavery, and the national struggles of the Civil War and the Civil Rights Movement, can profoundly overshadow the perceptions of contemporary Americans. Both sides in these conflicts made use of Scripture to justify their position (Eph 6:5; Col 3:22; Titus 2:9; Gal 3:28). This history could prevent an objective understanding of the social conditions in the first century when, as a result of Rome's imperial expansion, depending on who you read, up to sixty percent of the inhabitants of the empire are believed to have been enslaved. Either presumption, that the American experience of slavery or that the American capacity to overcome that system applied to slaves and masters in the first-century world also amounts to ethnocentrism, implies that the ancients should have perceived the injustice and overcome it, "just as we did." We will never understand Paul's motivations for sending Onesimus back to Philemon (Phlm 10-12) if we cannot divorce ourselves momentarily from our own experience and enter into Paul's world.

It is equally problematic to impose terminology borrowed or developed to describe specific practices in one society on another, distant in place or time. The term "taboo," for example, has been borrowed by some biblical scholars from the cultures of the South Pacific in attempts to make sense of the unique categories of "clean" and "unclean" in the religious consciousness of ancient Judaism. Close examination discloses, however, that the term is more obscuring than enlightening, introducing polytheistic concepts, motivations, and fears that have no place in Jewish religiosity.

Cultural Heterogeneity: More contemporary anthropology tends to discredit the assumption that cultures are homogeneous. Instead, it has been demonstrated that cultures are not neat packages comprised of set rules to which all are obedient, but are often muddled systems in which contradictory assumptions strive for ascendancy.[12] Having come to expect cultural heterogeneity, studies now actively seek out distinctions between social classes, genders, and practices of power and dominance.[13] The issue is not to discover class warfare, proletarian struggles, and the like, but to acknowledge that in any given culture there will be groups and subgroups with distinct perspectives. Thus it is a mistake to rush to judgment, accepting the first, the loudest, the richest, or even the most powerful voices as representative of the culture at large.

Men and women, the old and the young, those with access to resources and those without, those who exercise authority and those who are powerless may each, from their own perspective, view a given object, behavior, or law quite differently, and yet with full understanding as cultural insiders. It takes no effort to see that what one person understands as a fair and equitable redistribution of goods for the public welfare can easily be held by the next person as a resented, unjust taxation of the hardworking for the sake of the undeserving. Each generation has its own estimation of appropriate clothing for formal or casual occasions, including observations about acceptable hemlines and the like. The question, in this case, is not who is right, but coming to trace, where possible, how each position interrelates with the next. It would be a mistake to presume that the ones in charge, or the ones holding positions closer to our own, determine the true meaning of things.

For example, we encounter the laws on the jubilee year, requiring the return of all sold property and the release of the enslaved (Lev 25; 27:17-24;

---

[12]J. G. Peristiany and Julian Pitt-Rivers, "Introduction," *Honor and Grace in Anthropology* (New York: Cambridge University Press, 1992) 4.

[13]Clifford, "Partial Truths," 15; and "On Ethnographic Allegory," 109; J. G. Peristiany and Julian Pitt-Rivers, "Introduction," 4.

Num 36:4). The priest or synagogue leader might preach and teach these laws, and the peasant might yearn for their implementation, but that does not mean that the wealthy or powerful would observe them if rulers did not require it of them. In fact, we have few reasons beyond late attestation in the rabbinic writings to believe that the jubilee was often, if ever, observed. So then, we may well ask just what *was* the belief about the jubilee in the first century, and conclude that several voices could all speak differently, and *correctly*.

The discovery of the literature at Qumran, combined with what was already known concerning tensions between Pharisees and Sadducees, accompanying a further awareness and interest in Hellenism's tremendous impact, have all gone far to eradicate any sense of a monolithic Jewish culture in first-century Judaism. Further, what can be said of the whole, in this case, should also be extended to the parts. Indeed, even the Pharisees were not monolithic among themselves, as evidenced by the disputations between the schools of Hillel and Shammai, presuming uncertainly that they were Pharisees, and other debates among the rabbis from later Rabbinic literature.

Temporal Discontinuity: As a corollary to this point it is important to recognize different cultural periods at play within any given culture. Traditional, non-western societies are not static—they change. This may seem obvious to us in our radically changing times. Who could confuse the America of the Fifties with that of the Sixties and later? While some have proposed that so-called "primitive" cultures were conservative and stable rather than innovative and dynamic, evidence suggests, to the contrary, that non-technological societies, even conservative ones, adjust to new circumstances. Many factors prompt adaptation, including droughts, floods, disease, internal political shakeups, migrations and wars, new religious concepts, even artistic innovations.[14] Refusal to recognize this societal capacity for change, even in the most conservative of societies, leads inevitably to cultural oversimplification.

For example, it is problematic to equate the cultural world of ancient pre-exilic Israel with that of late-first-century Second Temple Judaism. There are several distinct periods reflecting profoundly divergent manifestations of communal, religious, and literary life, as is evidenced in the Hebrew Bible. These include, in simplistic form, a pre-monarchic period of loose tribal confederation, a shift to a centralized governance under a monarchy, a time of defeat and exile for the court and its retainers, and a period of return and reconstruction under a series of overlords, including Persians, Ptolemies, Seleucids, and Romans. At any one of these periods

---

[14]Moore, *Visions of Culture*, 204.

the distinct subcultures, including, among others, urban dwellers, rural farmers, the king's court, the priestly hierarchy, etc., shifted in different ways to adapt according to the extant pressures and events of their time. The same can be said for the religious movements such as the Pharisees, Sadducees, Essenes, and eventually the Christians and Zealots.

Romantic Historicism: Another perception to avoid is the one that exalts the cultural articulations from a culture's past, as their *true* expressions, as the *authentic* frames of reference, denigrating later expressions as devolutions. We can see that both the Deuteronomist and the Chronicler do this, exalting the reigns of David and Solomon. While it may be theologically convenient to be able to identify a particular age and way of life by which all others were to be judged, contemporary anthropological models discourage this approach as arbitrary and too subjective for critical discourse. In a constantly changing human society there has to be a more substantive reason for elevating as an apogee, or denigrating as a corruption, any particular time and place than the similarity it shares with our own philosophical or theological preferences or oppositions. Theological ethnocentrism is no less questionable simply because it is theological.[15]

Evaluations have been made by some who noticed similarities between later priestly concerns and practices of the Catholic and Orthodox churches. The Priestly writings were then denigrated or praised depending on the perceivers' points of view, not so much on the content of the work of the Priestly author, but on the critic's perception of Catholic liturgy or praxis. Therefore the determination that the Priestly literature of the Torah was a devolution from (or, equally, an evolutionary advance over) the more noble prophetic literature of a prior, more authentic age of true Israelite belief is anthropologically unsound.

In the first place, the elevation of earlier prophetic times over later priestly ones often sidesteps both how unhappy the prophets were with their own contemporaries and how energetically the prophetic teaching was maintained and observed by fervent post-exilic Jews. Second, one might well question whether the prophets themselves were truly representative of anybody's faith other than their own, since they often appeared to be isolated individuals or groups whose teachings seemed unattractive to the majority of their contemporaries. One might ask who reflected the prevailing belief and culture, the Deuteronomist and the few kings who succeeded

---

[15]For an outsider's perspective on how Christian ethnocentrism has distorted the interpretation of ancient Israel, Judaism, and the Scriptures see Howard Eilberg-Schwartz, *The Savage in Judaism: An Anthropology of Israelite Religion and Ancient Judaism* (Indianapolis: Indiana University Press, 1990) 49–86.

according to the Deuteronomic system of evaluation, or the much greater number of kings who worshiped in the high places and maintained the holy places scattered throughout Israel and Judah? Again, in summary, in a constantly changing human society there are no substantive anthropological grounds for elevating as an apogee, or denigrating as a corruption, any particular time and place even if it shares a similarity with our own philosophical or theological preferences or oppositions.

For that matter, the nostalgia for some older, purer, more authentic past is often revealed as a chimera. Behind every happier, prior place or lost authentic cultural expression or moment, is another point of perception with a similar lament for a still older way of doing and being, lost forever. The ultimate referent to the genuine culture was, of course, the putative culture conceived of and passed on by Eve to her children.[16]

The Economically Disadvantaged: In a deliberate attempt to avoid the terminology of "upper" and "lower" class, which is weighted in some circles to imply more than is intended here, we will refer to those who have access to economic resources and those who do not, with varying degrees of access between the two. Part of the process of dialogue with the ancient cultures of Palestine requires that we seek out evidence, not only of factional divisions, but of differentiation along the lines of economic production, social status, and gender.

In many cases only the wealthy minority have full access to the goods of their society and the time to pursue both education and leisurely pursuits. The poor and marginalized, however, often make up the overwhelming majority of any given populace. It has been the norm until fairly recently that few could read or write, apart from those who labored as scribes, with illiteracy in many cultures reaching up to ninety-five percent, depending on circumstances and dates. Thus in many societies the only ones with sufficient resources to produce literature and construct monumental buildings, that is, the literature we read from the ancients, including the Scriptures, and the buildings that remain for our archaeologists to excavate, the palaces and temples, often represent the thoughts and lifestyle of only a small portion of the populace.

It is imperative, however, that anthropologists studying past cultures not only access the more readily available evidence that comes to us from the elite minorities but seek out, in whatever ways possible, the voices of the often silent, less advantaged majority. Their lives are not always what we expect. Research on mummies, including the remains of the less advantaged,

---

[16]Raymond Williams, *The Country and the City* (New York: Oxford University Press, 1973) 9–12.

indicates that throughout its ancient history Egypt's people, advantaged and disadvantaged alike, were often beset by chronic anemia, an assortment of desert lung diseases and pneumonia, multiple parasitic infections, poor teeth, and the like. The disadvantaged added malnutrition and its resulting debilitations. It is presumed that nearly everyone lived with some form of severe pain and that most died by age thirty-five.[17] Studies of ancient Rome and Palestine suggest similar statistics. Poor water supplies were a particularly onerous problem, leading most to resort to brewing weak wine or beer for ordinary hydration, not for the intoxicating effects of the alcohol but because, though they may not have known it, the alcohol killed what was killing them. The poor Palestinian peasant consumed only about 1800 calories per day, of which approximately one quarter came from alcohol. Tragically, up to seventy-five percent of those who *survived* infant mortality died by the age of twenty-six.[18]

Thus even though the Scripture records life spans of "seventy years, or eighty for those who are strong" (Ps 90:10), this was almost certainly only the case for the few with access to what little health care existed and sufficient nutrition. When one considers these statistics and then rereads the overwhelming sense of desperation evident in Mark 1:30-38, where Jesus is mobbed by the sick and their attendants after he has cured Peter's mother-in-law, we can approach this scene with an entirely different level of understanding. These were not grasping people seeking a cheap cure but the desperate seeking hope where none had been expected.

To give a hierarchical example, the primarily cultic interest of the final Priestly redactors and authors of Torah, who had full access to the Temple and its rites, resulted in a definitive legal and religious text that spends a significant portion of its writing defining the manner in which purity at the Temple should be preserved. Much less time is spent considering the religious lives of the laity. It is only after considerable effort, seeking out multiply attested evidence from both Jewish and Gentile sources, that we are able to determine much about the religious lives of non-priestly Jews in Judea and throughout the Diaspora in the first century. We only then learn that they attempted to refrain from foods prohibited by Torah, and to observe the Sabbath, even when imperiled.[19]

[17]Brian Fagan, "Mummy Dearest: A Lost World Emerges From the Sands of Time," *Los Angeles Times* (Dec. 24, 2000) 6–7. Brian Fagan is an anthropologist at the University of California, Santa Barbara.

[18]Richard L. Rohrbaugh, *The Social Sciences and New Testament Interpretation* (Peabody, MA: Hendrickson, 1996) 4–5.

[19]Jacob Neusner, *The Idea of Purity in Ancient Israel* (Leiden: Brill, 1973) 30–31. Regarding the observance of the Sabbath see the following: Ovid [43 B.C.E.–18 C.E.], *Art of*

Recognizing distinctions of ownership and access to economic opportunities, however, is more than simply recounting the manner in which the
dominant, affluent, or educated viewed those with fewer resources. The
Tosephta, Megillah 2:7, informs us that priests were most holy. In de-
scending degrees of holiness were Levites, Israelites, converts, freed slaves,
disqualified priests, Temple slaves, bastards, eunuchs, men with damaged
testicles and those without a penis, who were least holy. It is an orderly
system with a clear hierarchical perspective. It is also questionable to the
degree that it does not inform us of the worldview and self-perception of
the lower ranks, such as the Temple slave, bastards, or eunuchs. Did they
either understand or accept their place on this scale? Would the Temple
slaves have considered themselves any less holy than the persons and insti-
tution they served, or did they see themselves outside the system altogether
with an independent means of evaluating their own importance? Who
can say? The *Tosephta* is representative of the elite perspective of well-
educated Rabbinic scholars, written in its final form long after the Temple
had ceased to exist. It is at least worth questioning whether its position
represented the self-perception of those occupying the lower stratum.

Inclusive Perspectives: One of the cultural elements requiring particular
attention in any given society is the different experiences and self-
expressions that surface concerning gender. Many cultures provide radically different experiences and opportunities along gender lines. Because it
is desirable to hear from every witness, it is important to include the voices
of women, though this entails two particularly troublesome difficulties.

First, a thorough student of the Scriptures needs to be wary of the sexist
presumptions of authoritative interpreters of biblical cultures, regrettably
even when reading experts in the field of ethnography. The classic example
of this involves the interpretation of the "enforced" sequestering of menstruating women of the Yuroks of California. The practice had been consistently interpreted by male anthropologists, from their interviews with male
Yuroks, as necessary to protect the males of the culture from the weakening
that inevitably results when men are polluted by menstrual blood. Since
weak men can neither hunt nor defend, it is imperative for menstruating

---

Love 1.413-16; Seneca the Younger [c. 4 B.C.E.–65 C.E.], *Concerning Superstition*, cited by
Augustine, *City of God* 6.11. For example, Strabo (ca. 64 B.C.E.–20 C.E.) recounts that
Pompey was able to seize the city of Jerusalem by "waiting for the day of fasting, when the
Judeans were abstaining from all work" (Strabo, *Geography* 16.2.40). There are other depic-
tions of the Jews being observant even to their own peril (see also Frontinus [ca. 40–104
C.E.], *Stratagems* 2.1.17; Plutarch [ca. 46–120 C.E.], *On Superstition* 8). These two examples
may, in turn, indicate a "general" positive accommodation to the prescriptions of Torah.

women to keep their distance. More recent studies, often by female ethnographers who practiced the novel approach of asking the *women* to explain their behavior, revealed the inadequacy of this understanding. For Yurok women the sequestering was a time of renewal when they did not have to clean, plant, reap, carry, or tend. It was not enforced by or for the sake of the men, but was something they did for their own spiritual renewal, renewing ties among themselves and reflecting on life.[20] Too often the voices of men are accepted uncritically as definitive and comprehensive by scholars when women, as in the case of the Yurok, have a different, equally valid witness to offer.

The second problem, even for the sensitive, inclusive investigator, is that even when the testimony of women is desired, many women are denied an opportunity to be heard. Due to the literary and architectural silence of women in some societies of the ancient world we are often blind to their participation in, or rejection of, the societal roles permitted them by men. Few women in the ancient world had access to the educational opportunities necessary for literacy. As a result, it is probably fair to assume that almost everything we read in the Scriptures is a reflection by men writing for and to other men, even when it concerns or interprets the activity of women. Men, then, chose which texts, of interest to them, would be preserved and collected in canons and distributed.

This leaves the anthropological endeavor uncomfortably lacking in female witnesses. Too often we cannot say with certainty whether most women were devoted to the same ancestral traditions as were described by men in the sacred texts, or if they implemented them for the same or different reasons, let alone shared the male interpretation of them. It is possible, even probable, that Israelite and Jewish women shared among themselves household pieties, practices, and concerns from great antiquity that were never voiced in the Scriptures. Mark 7:1-4 offers us the opportunity to consider the silent but active role of women in the washing of hands, cups, pots, jars, and bed linens (vv. 3-4). It seems unlikely, from what we know, that male heads of the household were doing these ritual cleansings or visiting the marketplace as the normal course. Regrettably, too often one can only wonder how the women of ancient Israel and Judea, if given a voice, would have recorded their piety and practices, the experience of menstruation or childbirth. One need not assume that written Scriptures represented their voices on the subject.

---

[20]Marvin Harris, *Culture, People, Nature: An Introduction to General Anthropology* (New York: Harper Collins College Publishers, 1993) 347.

Cultural Permeability: We will also need, as pointed out in the introduction, to give due attention to how cultures frequently lack a proper respect for geographical boundaries, interacting with each other in a manner that allows for more interconnectedness than has been traditionally allowed. Although people living within the same geographical locations often differ culturally, the seams and cracks are not as sharp in reality as would be convenient for the ethnographic enterprise.[21] The resulting gray areas make it difficult to establish the supposedly "authentic" elements of a given culture from the introduced practices and beliefs of its neighbors. This also challenges the position of some who insist on the uniqueness of Israel's religion. One need only consider the polemic behind the Deuteronomist's constant battle with the influence of "pagan" Baalism to recognize the real fluidity of Israel's culture and how profoundly it was affected by its neighbors.

Of more particular relevance to our study, Hellenism played a much more vital role in shaping Second Temple Judaism than has been credited in some research. It is critical, when comparing first-century C.E. Judaism to the Hellenistic world around it, to recognize the considerable overlap between the two.[22] Since the time of Alexander the Great, Judea had been enveloped in a larger cultural milieu from which it could not remain isolated. Jews in the Diaspora, and even in Judea though to a lesser extent, were necessarily Hellenized.[23] The very names of the Hasmoneans—Aristobulus, Alexander, Alexandra, etc.—whose family rose to prominence as the great defenders of Judaism from the encroachments of Hellenism, evidenced that they themselves were drawn to it in time.

Societal Distinctiveness: Recognizing the complexity of the question of interaction between neighboring cultures and in no way negating the prior point, we must also come to grips with the opposing dictum that customs shared by different ethnic groups, *even neighboring ones*, do not always stem from the same root causes. Parallels between adjacent cultures may actually be based on divergent, immediately local phenomena, and not related to the root causes of their neighbors' behaviors. The following two points are important: (1) in essence, differing personalities, events, or conditions can lead to identical behavior; (2) conversely, identical conditions can also lead to diverging responses. Before arriving at any

---

[21]Matthews and Benjamin, "Introduction: Social Sciences and Biblical Studies," 16.

[22]Shaye J. D. Cohen, *Maccabees to the Mishnah* (Philadelphia: Westminster, 1987) 34–45.

[23]Martin Hengel, *Judaism and Hellenism*, 2 vols. (Philadelphia: Fortress, 1974) 1:103–106.

conclusions of a particular similarity between Israel's, or later, Judea's, culture and that of its neighbors, it is necessary to trace the development of the given practice separately, in each culture, in order to identify either commonality or differentiation. Before undertaking such a task one would do well to justify its necessity. Biblical researchers in particular should question the need for either maintaining the uniqueness of Israel or blaming its faults on corruptions from exterior influences. Once a behavior becomes part of the culture, whether or not its origins were indigenous, it is as authentic as it is widely and freely practiced.

Systemic Perspective: On a different track, we would do well to be aware of the tremendous interrelatedness of religion and its symbols with the other elements of culture, including the overall structure of a society, its history and ends. Though religious texts like the Bible may focus largely on sacred matters while neglecting the other elements of culture, the practice of religion remains intimately connected to them, whether in support of the larger political and social systems or in opposition to them.[24]

Judaism, by the time of Christ, was already an ancient, substantial, and complex religion, whose practices and beliefs were profoundly impacted by its long role as the primary spiritual expression of the Israelite and Judean peoples. The shift from an independent monarchy to a province, the exile to Babylon, the pressures of the pervasive Hellenistic culture, political subjection to Egypt, Syria, and Rome, the reconstruction of the Temple by Herod, the proximity of significant numbers of nonbelievers, the effects of the climate on the production of food, and many other significant events in the history of the social life of Israel and Judea can be shown to have had profound impact on the religion in subsequent centuries.

The concern for the preservation of religion and culture in Judea, the need to separate Roman from Temple coinage at the Temple, the separation of different groupings of priests, laymen, laywomen, and Gentiles in the various courts while at the Temple, and the concern for appropriate table fellowship can all be seen as products of historically distinctive forces. In essence, the religion of Israel and Judah did not exist in a vacuum. It both produced and was a product of the national life, with all the components from which its culture was derived.

The interrelatedness of cultural elements does not mean, however, that every element in culture is *functional* per se. Some elements of culture meet other adaptive requisites of human existence, including those that express in the broadest strokes the creativity of human actors in their use of

---

[24]Talal Asad, *Genealogies of Religion* (Baltimore: Johns Hopkins University Press, 1993) 54.

symbols. One should be hesitant, therefore, to speak too quickly of the purpose of a particular cultural construct, some of which may have no ends beyond self-expression.[25]

Labels: Objectivity suggests that ethnographers refrain from ethnocentric or racist assessments of other cultures. This includes use of evaluative terminology, either positive or pejorative, such as "primitive," "advanced," "savage," "noble," "barbaric," and the like. Judgments of superiority or inferiority are not helpful in establishing understanding.[26]

Members of European and American cultures have no grounds for establishing their own culture as a standard by which others are to be judged. Just as in the case of metaphorical interpretation, these labels obscure as much as they enlighten. Which is the "advanced" society, the one that enables great technological advances while trampling the environment, or the one that lives without the medical and scientific advantages but abides in harmony with nature? Which is the noble society, the one that celebrates human freedom while allowing women and children to live in an endless cycle of poverty, or the one that constrains human freedom yet succeeds in meeting the needs of every member? In each of these cases, though they are "hypothetical," it would be better simply to describe the conditions of the society than to engage in evaluative judgments.

In the same way there is nothing gained and sometimes much lost in the practice of providing pejorative labels for either Jews or their neighbors. Groups such as the Canaanites and the Phoenicians have often been labeled "pagan." Denigrating the Canaanites in no way ennobles Israel. The terrible price paid by Jews for the Christian practice of equating Pharisees with shallow, legalistic hypocrites became a source of horror in the last century, highlighting the worst case of the misuse of evaluative language and its consequences.

The Emic and the Etic: While we are stressing the importance of the sympathetic insider to understanding, not everything claimed by such witnesses is taken without a healthy critical investigation. Anthropologists make an important distinction between what is referred to as the "emic" and the "etic."

The first, the emic, is the manner in which a culture describes its motivations and how things ought to be. The second, the etic, is the description of the culture's actual practices as apparent to the perceptive observer. The difference between the two is that the first issues normative statements of value and the second describes observable behavior or practice. The

[25]Moore, *Visions of Culture,* 274.
[26]Matthews and Benjamin, "Introduction: Social Sciences and Biblical Studies," 15.

distinction arises from the pragmatic anthropological insight that what representatives of a culture say they do or believe may diverge from what an outsider observes them doing, and what they can be shown to believe. The actual social relationships of a culture, particularly in their public practice, tend to vary from their stated norms.[27]

While one should expect an interrelation of cultural elements, one may find that an occasional cultural aspect is hard to include within the larger framework. One can expect a certain amount of inconsistency in almost all cultures, and that some of the incongruities will not be easily explained either by local conditions or by neighboring influences. Culture is neither accurately pieced together in fragments nor always a smoothly integrated body.

We can readily see this in the contrast found in the United States between what is found in the Declaration of Independence concerning "life, liberty, and the pursuit of happiness," with its concomitant description of America as "the land of the free," and the African-American experience of living in America. Slavery, restricted neighborhoods, constrained work opportunities, and segregated churches, restaurants, schools, and colleges do not necessarily belie the experience of freedom for those who originate from Europe. They *do,* however, indicate that more than one experience may not cohere with the national self-perception. America *has been* a land where some have been free, but not all.

It can be readily observed that not all Catholics refrain from eating meat on Fridays in Lent, even though their church requires it, nor do all Jews and Christians refrain from adultery although such behavior is specifically, scripturally and ecclesially, prohibited.

Students of the Bible would do well to consider that texts intended for didactic or inspirational purposes, such as the Bible, tend to emphasize the normative, emic point of view. What can be said of other emic expressions can be said of the Bible as well: one cannot presume that all the teachings contained in it were observed by every member of the societies who produced it.

We read a classic emic description of the life of the early Christian community in Acts 2:42-47, where all life and goods were shared in common, great signs were worked, and the community "devoted themselves to the teaching of the apostles and to the communal life, to the breaking of the bread and to the prayers." Everything appears to have been idyllic and

---

[27]John K. Chance, "The Anthropology of Honor and Shame: Culture, Values, and Practice," *Semeia* 68 (1994) 146.

harmonious. In Acts 5:1-11, however, we can observe that at least two in the community, Ananias and Sapphira, were *not* sharing all in common, and were then lying about it. Again, in Acts 6:1 we read that the Greek-speaking Jewish Christian widows were neglected in the sharing of the community's daily distribution. An etic observation on the overly positive emic perspective of Acts 2:42-47 is that the early Christian community valued its life in common and strove to live in harmony, but had to struggle with dishonesty, hoarding, and ethnic prejudice.

What can be said of a culture as a whole can be said of its constituent parts, including individuals. Paul, in Rom 12:9-18, extols the values of living together in mutual affection, showing each other honor and, where possible, living at peace with everyone. This is the same writer who, when writing to the Galatians, refers to them as stupid and bewitched (Gal 3:1), suggesting that they castrate those in their midst who are proponents of circumcision (Gal 5:12).

Conformity and Eccentricity: This last point demands that we be attentive to the question of how much conformity we can expect from the people who make up a given culture. While careful study is able to provide us with broad generalities on particular societies, individuals within that society can conform completely, reflect only partial cooperation with the other members of their society, be constructive agents of peaceful change, or rebel utterly. In effect, we find that individuals cannot be summed up by their cultural origins.

In our own world, did Cesar Chavez fit the profile of an uneducated, originally undocumented, seasonal laborer from Mexico? Do not some well-reared children from affluent, loving families become rabbis, ministers, nuns, and priests, while others—sometimes even from the same family—become face-painting heavy metal band members? Whenever you deal with humans, you can expect some element of nonconformity.

It is not enough to summarize the individuals producing or portrayed in Scripture by identifying their cultural matrix. When Nathaniel asked concerning Jesus, "Can anything good come from Nazareth?" (John 1:46) he made the incorrect presumption that individuals are simply products of their environments. There is a complex dialectical process between individuals and their cultures. Individuals both shape and are shaped by their cultures of origin. Some rebel altogether.

We could well ask if the Scriptures indicate that Jesus was a typical Jew. The answer would be both "yes" and "no." At times he conformed, observing the Sabbath (Luke 4:16), wearing the distinctively Jewish tassels required by the Law (Matt 9:20; Num 15:28; Deut 22:12), and publicly celebrating the great Jewish feasts (Mark 14:12-13; John 2:23). At others, he seemed to be at odds, distancing himself from his family (Mark 3:31-35), neglecting the ordinary daily meal practices (Luke 11:38), and offending his religious peers (Matt 23:13-35). He both insists on the observance of the Law (Matt 5:17-19) and gives what appear to be creative interpretations of it (Matt 5:21-48).

In summary, an anthropological consciousness is a useful tool in biblical studies precisely because it cautions us to approach sympathetically, listen carefully and to as many witnesses as possible, and to judge sparingly. Such a consciousness, to be truly affective in studying the Scriptures, must be accompanied by a broad exposure to the available evidence found in contemporary non-Scriptural writings, epigraphical inscriptions, archaeology remains of buildings, tombs, and, curiously, trash heaps, etc. Admittedly, approaching the Scriptures in this fashion requires significant background study and precludes an easy, casual reading of a passage but, as our study of Luke 7:36-50 will hopefully demonstrate, such an endeavor is worth the time and effort in the abundance of new insights and interpretations it brings to each text.

CHAPTER THREE

The Cultural Worlds of Jesus and Simon the Pharisee

Having perused, lightly, a number of attitudes and approaches for maintaining an anthropological consciousness, we can now apply them to our study of Luke 7:36-50. This task is complicated, though, since the text reflects input from more than one culture. In the first place, we have the cultural world supposedly described by the text, but we also have the cultural world of the author of the text as we have it now. Each needs careful consideration. To accomplish this we will consider these two worlds in sequence, beginning with Jesus' and Simon's non-elite social context in a first-century Galilean milieu, from which Luke's earliest traditions seem to have been drawn.

This world will be difficult to uncover. Unfortunately, subsistence farmers and simple town folk were largely illiterate and left few literary clues about their daily lives. Their elite, affluent, and well-educated contemporaries, who constituted only a small portion of the general populace but produced almost all of the literature, were largely uninterested in the daily, often brutish lives of peasants, and so made little effort to record their practices and beliefs. These peasants, unlike the elite who built homes and public buildings out of stone, often constructed their buildings out of mud bricks and plant materials that decay quickly when not carefully maintained. Thus the peasants, who formed the largest portion of their societies, often left little trace of their passing beyond the pottery they used and the rough stone foundations of their buildings.

This leaves us at a distinct disadvantage as we seek to engage this society as sympathetic insiders. In fact, often the best windows into this cultural world remain the gospels and Acts of the Apostles. "Best," however, does not necessarily mean reliable. Upon investigation most serious scholars conclude that few if any of the final authors and editors of the

New Testament were insiders from the Judean peasant culture about which the evangelists wrote. Even Paul was supposedly from Tarsus (Acts 21:39; 22:3), not Judea. At times it will be difficult to distinguish accurate descriptions from uninformed guesswork and misconceptions, since these early traditions come to us altered by the storytelling capacities and purposes of subsequent reporters. To be clear on this point, as Chapter One indicated, most scholars conclude that the gospels were not eyewitness reports. Between the events and teachings of the life of Jesus and the recording of them in the gospels there was a time of telling, retelling, and adaptation of these earlier traditions, both in and outside of Judea, according to the needs of developing Christian communities. Only later were they incorporated by the evangelists into their gospels.

At this point it would be good to do a slow, careful, attentive reading of Luke 7:36-50 and the preceding and following chapters to be able to place this event in its context, considering carefully the characters who inhabit its given setting, their social roles, and their activities in the narrative. The text describes a meal in the home of Simon, a Pharisee, to which Jesus, a Jew raised in Galilee, is invited. Luke does not clarify the location of Simon's house, although Jesus would appear to be still in Galilee and perhaps even in Nain, his last identified location (Luke 7:11), since he does not seem to have moved from there. There is a question in Simon's mind about the possibility that Jesus is a prophet. His invitation to Jesus to join him at dinner and his eventual disappointed evaluation of Jesus as "not a prophet" are the real prompts that initiate the critical interplay between him and Jesus.

The Pharisees

Because of the importance of Simon as a character in this narrative and of his home as the setting, we will study the Pharisees in a focused way, and only then address how Luke portrayed them in his gospel. Although there are other entrance points for an anthropological study of Luke 7:36-50, this book will use the Pharisees as a sample case study for demonstrating the difficulty of and the reward for investigating the cultural side of biblical texts.

As important as Pharisees were in the narratives of the New Testament, they amply demonstrate that there is, unfortunately, less concrete evidence from the first century than one might desire when attempting to accurately depict life at that time. Historically, the later decades of the first century were very tumultuous. Hostility toward Rome, its policies and taxes, led to open rebellion in the sixties. The Romans responded ruthlessly, destroying

Jerusalem, its Temple, and much of the countryside by the year 70 C.E. These events drastically changed the face of Judaism, depriving the chief priests of their central position in the life of worship, destroying the quasi-monastic communities of the Essenes, and upsetting the political balance that had operated in the decades prior to the revolt. An unfortunate side effect of these events is that the literature of Jerusalem and Palestine was destroyed in the sacking. Some literary evidence remains, including the various documents in the New Testament, the writings of Josephus, a late-first-century Jewish historian, some extracanonical religious writings, including the various documents found at Qumran, and traditions that survive in later Jewish writings, such as the Mishnah.

The most desirable source on the Pharisees would be their own writing, particularly if they wrote about themselves, their lives, values, customs, and beliefs. Unfortunately, even if they had produced such writings, they either no longer exist or are up to this point impossible to identify. Various texts have been presumed to be about them or attributed to them, the Mishnah being the most important example of the latter, but scholarly opinion is contested in each case.[1]

It is remarkable in itself how few clearly, reliably identifiable Pharisees there are. Pre-fourth-century C.E. literature only identifies about a dozen individuals, and usually not in particularly instructive circumstances for our purposes.[2] No woman, named or otherwise, is ever included among them, though some would include the unique figure of Queen Salome Alexandra, who ruled Judea briefly, from 76 to 67 B.C.E., after the death of her husband, Alexander Janneus.[3] Some of the twelve named individuals

---

[1] These include disputed allusions to the Pharisees in Ezra, Nehemiah, and Malachi, and attributions of entire works to them, such as the *Psalms of Solomon,* the *Assumption of Moses, Jubilees,* and even the *Damascus Document* (CD); see Steve Mason, *Flavius Josephus on the Pharisees* (Boston: Brill Academic Publishers, 1991) 7–10.

[2] One list includes Eleazar (a contemporary of John Hyrcanus and possibly a Pharisee, *Ant.* 13.288-298), Pollion the Pharisee (*Ant.* 14.172-176; 15.3-4), Saddock (the cofounder with Judas the Galilean of Josephus' Fourth Philosophy; *Ant.* 18.4), Simon the Pharisee (Luke 7:36-50), Nicodemus (John 3:1-15; 7:50-52; 19:39), Paul (Phil 3:5-6; Gal 1:14; Acts 23:6), Paul's alleged teacher, Gamaliel (Acts 5:34-39; 22:3), Flavius Josephus (*Life* 12), Simon ben Gamaliel (*Life* 191–192), the priest Jozar (*War* 2.628; *Life* 63, 73), Jonathan and Ananias (members of a delegation sent to depose Josephus; *Life* 197; *War* 2.451, 2.628); from Joseph Sievers, "Who Were the Pharisees?" in James H. Charlesworth and Loren L. Johns, eds., *Hillel and Jesus: Comparative Studies of Two Major Religious Leaders* (Minneapolis: Fortress, 1997) 138–53.

[3] Ibid. 153; Josephus, *War* 1.107-119. For more on the fascinating women who were influential among the elite of Second Temple Judaism, be sure to read the companion volume in this series by Florence Morgan Gillman, *Herodias: At Home in That Fox's Den* (Collegeville: Liturgical Press, 2003).

were scoundrels, some were men of great integrity, many of them were politically active, while some, including Josephus, were revolutionaries. With two exceptions they did not record their beliefs in any systematic way.[4] Unfortunately those two exceptions, Paul and Josephus, cannot be counted on as representatives of mainstream Pharisaic thought. Paul only mentions the Pharisees once, when he admits that he had been one himself: "Circumcised on the eighth day, a member of the people of Israel, of the tribe of Benjamin, a Hebrew born of Hebrews; as to the law, a Pharisee; as to zeal, a persecutor of the church; as to righteousness under the law, blameless" (Phil 3:5). In spite of this he had nothing to say about them. His letters, Romans and Galatians in particular, seem to reject any necessity for observing practices that appear dear to Pharisees in the gospels, clearly indicating he had left the movement before he began writing. Josephus, too, alludes to his own membership in the Pharisaic movement, but his position on them remains controversial since he often portrays Pharisees in a less than positive light.[5] Thus there is only disputed access to the Pharisees' self-understanding, the normal starting point for a cultural investigation.

As for the majority of the Pharisees, they seem, uncertainly, to have originated among village folk, and the humbler classes of the cities and towns. The paucity of witnesses from a movement described by both the New Testament and Josephus as originating in and popular among the common folk is not as surprising as it might first appear. The earliest references to a "canon" of their beliefs indicate, unsurprisingly, an oral rather than a written tradition. Since oral traditions are easily lost, this inevitably contributed to the paucity of self-reporting. Also, to reiterate, first-century non-elites had few means for preserving their thoughts for posterity. The survival of the New Testament, so much of which seems to have been produced by and for the serving and peasant classes, is the greater surprise and was dependent on the survival and religious motivations of the early church. To some extent something similar might be said of the second-century Jewish document, the Mishnah, although the scribal and rabbinic classes that produced it would be considered "privileged," at least within the Jewish subculture of the larger Greco-Roman world. Josephus' writings reflect the perspectives of an elite individual, writing for the edification of other members of his class, and for this reason probably had the greatest chance for survival into the modern world.

---

[4] Jacob Neusner, *The Rabbinic Traditions about the Pharisees before 70* (Leiden: Brill, 1971) 1:364–67.

[5] Mason, *Flavius Josephus on the Pharisees.*

Although the Pharisees had one brief window of political influence in the time of Salome Alexandra, after that time their greatest influence seems to have been over the politically least important rural segment of society.[6] Even if they were, in fact, the springboard for the movement that produced the Mishnah, and that is debated, they would only have come to any large scale predominance among Jews after the destruction of Jerusalem and its Temple. With the demolition of the Temple those priestly groups most focused on the Temple, its operation and status as the heart of Jewish religiosity, lost the ground for their continued existence. This would include the affluent and apparently influential Sadducees, from whose number were drawn some of the high priests, and the politically disenfranchised Essenes who directed much of their religious energy to "regaining" control of the Temple and "returning" it to proper use. Without the focal point of the Temple around which they operated they ceased to exist. The Pharisees appear to have directed their energies to lay observances in the home and the broader application of Temple and priestly ritual and cultic concerns in the lives of the laity.[7] In fact, it could be said that they offered a vision of Judaism that did not strictly require the existence of a Temple, but could flourish in homes and synagogues. Though they, too, seem to fade from public view, this may not be as it appears. It has been proposed that consolidation for the sake of survival led the bulk of observant Judaism into the Pharisaic camp by virtue of a vacuum—there were no other successful, adaptive Jewish expressions to embrace. If *mainstream* Judaism became identified with Pharisaism, the title "Pharisee," implying "set apart," could be dropped as unnecessary in the absence of non-Pharisaic Jews from which others needed to distinguish themselves.[8] As a result, some of the voices of early second-century Judaism, recorded in the Mishnah, may have been Pharisaic in their beliefs. This is an attractive hypothesis, but it has proved difficult to demonstrate it convincingly.

As a side note, what has been said about the difficulty of identifying Pharisees can also be said of the other major movements of the day. While

---

[6] The portrayal of their one involvement in politics by Josephus is not a favorable one, in that they used a truly pious woman, Alexandra, for political ends, ruthlessly destroying their enemies and tarnishing Alexandra's reign (*War* 1.110-114).

[7] Jacob Neusner, *Purity in Rabbinic Judaism: A Systematic Account* (Atlanta: Scholars, 1994) 109. The majority view is that most Pharisees were lay; see Joachim Jeremias, *Jerusalem in the Time of Jesus* (Philadelphia: Fortress, 1978) 257–59. Günter Stemberger finds contrary evidence that there may have been considerable priestly influence on the post-70 Rabbinic movement; see his *Jewish Contemporaries of Jesus* (Minneapolis: Fortress, 1995) 140–47.

[8] Marcel Simon, *Jewish Sects at the Time of Jesus* (Philadelphia: Fortress, 1967) 29.

four Essenes are named by Josephus, none was ever named in either the New Testament or Rabbinic literature. As for Sadducees, Josephus names two. The New Testament says that a high priest had an entourage of Sadducees (Acts 5:17). Thus while admittedly few Pharisees were ever named, in perspective only Christianity had more identified members among known Jewish groups active before the destruction of the Temple.[9]

There are, then, three extant primary literary sources for information on the practices and beliefs of the Pharisees to help us reconstruct the part that Pharisees played in the cultural world of first-century Judaism. These include the New Testament, the writings of Josephus, and possibly the Mishnah.

The New Testament offers us a treasury of references to the Pharisees, being far and away the richest and earliest source, with allusions to them in six of its writings. The two earliest of these among extant texts are Paul's letter to the Philippians, composed between 50 and 52 C.E., and the Gospel of Mark, presumed written between 65 and 72 C.E. The other gospels, Matthew, Luke, and John, and the Acts of the Apostles also mention the Pharisees. The majority of biblical scholars presume that these New Testament narratives were composed between 80 and 100 C.E. Unfortunately, by far the greatest number of references describe their interaction with Jesus and his disciples, and fail to outline their beliefs.

Roughly contemporary with them are the writings of Josephus ben Matthias, a first-century Jewish historian (37–100 C.E.). According to his own self report Josephus was born into a priestly family; in his nineteenth year, after flirting with the Essene movement, he lived according to the Pharisaic way of life. Three of his four extant writings mention the Pharisees, including *The Jewish War* (75–80 C.E.), *The Antiquities of the Jews* (90–95 C.E.), and his *Life* (95–100 C.E.). Of all our sources his are the most intentionally historical, based on a first-hand experience of Pharisees and their way of life.

The remaining source of information on the Pharisees is the Mishnah, a collection of short religious tracts on a variety of religious subjects pertinent to Judaism that reached its final form relatively late, about the year 200 C.E. A large portion of its content is attributed to religious leaders, some of them Pharisees, who lived both before and after Jesus.

Unfortunately, as will become clear, the utility of each is severely compromised for different reasons. As we shall see, each of these three sources offers us qualified information on the Pharisees that cannot always

[9] Sievers, "Who Were the Pharisees?" 154.

be assumed to be "historically objective," at least as we have come to understand the concept.

The New Testament

There are important cautions that should be kept in mind about the use of the New Testament as a source concerning the Pharisees. First, it should be noted that the dating and location of the final composition of the New Testament texts that refer to them place them outside the immediate cultural milieu of Palestine. It is not certain whether all the gospel writers had ever encountered Pharisees, or whether some were completely dependent on their sources for information about them.

Although it is certain that the gospels and Acts contain traditions of events and beliefs that can be traced to Palestine, it is also true that they were often filtered through second- or even third-hand perspectives, shaped by interests other than representing Palestine, its cultures, or, in particular, the Pharisees. When the authors of the New Testament set out to write they did not include representing an historically accurate, full, and orderly representation of Pharisaic belief or practice among their goals. Rather, the Pharisees served a number of literary purposes. They enabled the authors to amplify the importance of certain topics by having them introduced in the midst of disagreement. They gave readers the opportunity to see Jesus' teachings clarified by their contrast with other positions, leading them to understand the far-reaching consequences of the choices the early Christians needed to make. They also served as warnings to members of the church of the behaviors they would need to avoid. In essence, the Pharisees often appear to have been foils for the authors' greater interest in portraying the life and teachings of Jesus.[10]

It is important to keep in mind, though, that the early Christians' perceptions of the world around them, accurate or not, whether historical or founded on sectarian animosity, determined their reactions and participated in the formation of their faith. The manner in which the early Christians perceived the Pharisees and their own relationship to them is, for some of our purposes, as important as our own modern, scholarly, and historical perspective on them. That perception appears to have been clearly polemical.

Polemical discussions are problematic sources for ethnographic or cultural source material since they seldom offer objective material. The overpowering instincts of self-preservation, to defend and attack, create a

[10] Robert C. Tannehill, "Should We Love Simon the Pharisee?" *CurTM* 21 (1994) 426.

situation in which the participants often find impartiality beyond their reach. The New Testament's overtly belligerent, confrontational outsiders' perspectives on the Pharisees are clearly symptomatic of this polemic style. For our purposes this markedly hostile, anti-Pharisaic tone portrayed in every gospel, but particularly Matthew and John, needs to be admitted directly.

The gospels claim that Pharisees abused their authority over the synagogues (John 12:42-43), where their legal applications were hard-hearted (Mark 3:1-6; 10:3//Matt 19:8). In accordance with their legalistic mindset (Mark 2:24//Matt 12:2//Luke 12:2), they placed observance of the Law above the welfare of the sick.[11] Observing their ancestral traditions with greater care than explicit divine laws, they were hypocrites, giving God lip-service.[12] In fact, they did legal gymnastics about unimportant details, "filtering out the midge," all the while disregarding the truly weightier things of the Law, such as judgment, love for God, mercy, and fidelity, that is, "gulping down the camel" (Matt 23:23; Luke 11:42).

Their relationship with Jesus was particularly troubled since they feared his success, noting from the beginning how influential he was with the people, and suspected that his success could only be to their detriment (John 4:1-3; 7:31-32; 12:19), with terrible political and social consequences (John 11:45-48). The Pharisees tested Jesus[13] and requested that he rein in his disciples' messianic enthusiasm (Luke 19:38-40). Along with the chief priests they convened the Sanhedrin (John 11:47) and sought to have Jesus charged or arrested.[14] They were only prevented from doing so because they feared the crowds (Matt 21:45). Even so, they laid traps for him, hoping to trip him up publicly.[15] Sometimes alone, and sometimes in counsel with the Herodians, they plotted Jesus' death.[16] Eventually, when the time was right, the Pharisees joined with the chief priests in sending guards to arrest Jesus in the garden (John 18:3). Although they were markedly absent from the trial and crucifixion, after Jesus' death the Pharisees, again cooperating with the chief priests, tried to prevent the early Christians from pretending that Jesus was raised from the dead by stealing his body (Matt 27:62-66).

In contrast to Jesus they were pastoral failures, preaching what they did not practice, making religious observances difficult for others without

[11] Mark 3:6//Matt 12:14//Luke 6:7-11.
[12] Mark 7:6-13//Matt 15:3-10; 23:13, 15, 23, 29.
[13] Mark 8:11; 10:2//Matt 19:3; Matt 16:1; 22:34-40; John 8:6.
[14] Matt 21:45; John 7:31-32, 44-53; 8:6; 11:57.
[15] Mark 12:13//Matt 22:15; Matt 21:15; Luke 11:53-54; John 8:6.
[16] Mark 3:6//Matt 12:14//Luke 6:7-11; Luke 11:53-54.

helping them (Matt 23:1-4), closing heaven to others and not entering it themselves (Matt 23:13). They turned their converts into people worse than they were themselves (Matt 23:15). They escorted others toward the same pit into which they themselves were tumbling (Matt 15:14). Their righteousness was simply insufficient for the heavenly kingdom (Matt 5:20).

The gospels contain several powerful, negative analogies for the Pharisees. They were like a tree that, having failed to bear good fruit, was waiting to be cut down and destroyed (Matt 3:10), like a plant not sown by God waiting to be uprooted (Matt 15:13). They were blind (Matt 23:16; John 9:40-41), unable to read the signs of the times (Matt 16:2-3). They were an evil and unfaithful generation (Matt 12:39; 16:4). They were a brood of vipers (Matt 3:7; 12:34; 23:33).

The gospels claim that Pharisees were inclined to judge others according to outward impressions (John 8:15), and to invest too much effort in their own exteriors. All their works were performed to be seen by others, including their wearing of exaggeratedly large religious garments (Matt 23:5). They preferred places of honor, prestige, recognition in public places (Matt 23:7//Luke 11:43; 14:7-8), and titles of respect (Matt 23:7), refusing to consort with others more fallible than themselves (Matt 9:13). The fanfare was all for show, though. While maintaining their outward show of purity they were inwardly full of plunder and self-indulgence (Matt 23:25). They were like whitewashed tombs, deceptively attractive, but filled with the remnants of human decay and every kind of uncleanness, a source of defilement for those who did not comprehend them (Matt 23:27; Luke 11:44). Though they might succeed in fooling the masses, however, God was not fooled (Luke 16:15).

Because they had rejected God's plan for them (Luke 7:29-30), judgment was coming upon them. They had been invited by God to participate in the kingdom of heaven but had chosen not to participate (Matt 21:45–22:15). It was questionable whether they could escape the judgment of Gehenna (Matt 23:33). Thus the kingdom of God was taken away from the Pharisees and handed over to a people (the early church?) that would bear fruit (Matt 23:43-45). The best advice, as the early Christians saw things, was to beware of the Pharisees, their influence (Mark 8:15), their teaching (Matt 16:6, 11-12), and their hypocrisy (Luke 12:1).

What explains this all but unrelentingly negative portrayal? In part it was certainly due to a sense of inferiority, surprising as this may seem. The Pharisees were established and respected before Christianity surfaced. As the newcomers, early Christians apparently perceived that they were compared with Pharisees by other Jews, including the disciples of John, and not always favorably (Mark 2:18//Luke 5:33//Matt 9:14). There can be no doubt that the Pharisees found the observance of the Law wanting (Mark 2:16//Matt 9:11//Luke 5:30; Luke 15:4). In itself this might explain tension, but it would hardly be sufficient to provoke the passionate contempt of the New Testament, especially since so much of the New Testament's portrayal stands in tension with the best knowledge we have of first- and second-century Judaism.

In the first place, the Pharisees seem to have been very popular with the majority of Jews. While Josephus only places the number of the Pharisees at something over six thousand (*Ant.* 17.42) at a time when the population of Jerusalem is understood to have numbered around eighty thousand, he has many passages that indicate that the Pharisees had harmonious relationships with the general populace (*War* 2.166).[17] Their influence over the populace was such that they were believed even when they spoke out against kings or priests (*Ant.* 13.288) and were even able to persuade the populace to support the tenuous claim to the throne of Judea's only queen (*Ant.* 13.400-402). Their popularity so surpassed that of the Sadducees (*Ant.* 13.298) that public worship was conducted according to their guidance (*Ant.* 18.15). Josephus may have had his own reasons for portraying the Pharisees as popular with the masses, but reading between the lines there is even evidence to support that position in the New Testament. That Pharisees were fond of public recognition and titles of honor (Matt 23:6-7//Luke 11:43) suggests that they, in fact, received some degree of public respect. To whatever extent Josephus' claim of Pharisaic popularity was true, we are forced to ask: how true are the New Testament portrayals of them as unpleasant, self-righteous, hypocritical schemers? It is difficult to imagine how such a movement could have survived, let alone been successful and adaptive, or had the influence over late-first-century Judaism that many competent and respected scholars suggest it had. These scholars believe the Pharisees were largely influential in helping Judaism make the transition from a Temple-centered to a home-centered religion after the Jerusalem Temple was destroyed by the Romans in 70 C.E. The success of their movement, not by coercion but by persuasion—a success, in fact, far surpassing Christianity's smaller accomplishments among first-century Jews—belies much of the disapproving New Testament portrayal and may go far in explaining the very hostile tone we detect with such ease.

---

[17] It has been suggested that this passage may appear to be favorable at first glance, but if one were to compare this with the much more positive evaluation of the Essenes one might conclude that Josephus had dismissed the Pharisees with faint praise (Mason, *Flavius Josephus on the Pharisees,* 132). In light of the expressly hostile evaluation of the Sadducees that follows, however, this position is unduly negative. Josephus was apparently forced to admit that the Pharisees were on good terms with the general populace because it was true.

Another point to address is the peculiar disjunction in the New Testament portrayal of the Pharisees in which they emerge throughout Jesus' life and ministry, questioning and disputing, disapproving and even plotting, but disappear from the narrative before his trial, condemnation, suffering, and death, seemingly having played no significant part in it.[18] Mark, in particular, represents them as conspiring with the Herodians to put Jesus to death at an early point in the gospel (Mark 3:6). Conversely, in Matthew, Mark, and Luke the chief priests and the Sanhedrin played no part in Jesus' life and ministry and yet were directly responsible for his trial and execution.[19]

Why would the Pharisees, and their antagonism toward Jesus, play such an important part in the narrative of the gospels, heightening the tension and building toward the climactic scenes of judgment and condemnation, only to disappear before his downfall, in which they did not participate? It is possible that the disappearance of the Pharisees from the trial scenes may simply have reflected their limited influence in the political arena at this particular point in history. I tend to agree, though, with those who suggest that the depiction of constant antagonism in the gospels reflects more the relationship existing between Christians and Pharisees in 70 C.E. and beyond than it does the events in the life of Jesus.[20]

It is widely held by scholars that the trial and Passion accounts, containing the important involvement of the chief priests and the Sanhedrin, were among the earliest traditions put into narrative form. Only later were other traditions of Jesus' ministry and sayings, containing the participation of the Pharisees, shaped into their narratives by Matthew, Mark, and Luke and prefixed to their trial and Passion accounts. Always desiring to reconstruct the historical reality lying behind the early church traditions formalized in the gospels, scholars have proposed that the historical Jesus' real conflict lay not with the Pharisees at all, but with the Temple leadership in Jerusalem, who had the unenviable task of maintaining order in the Temple, the flashpoint of all Jewish aspirations for political and religious self-governance.

The first time the Temple leadership or the Sanhedrin had any reason to pay attention to Jesus, who was from their perspective an upstart hayseed

---

[18] In their last appearance, according to the less than credible tradition in John 18:3, they cooperate with Judas and the chief priests in sending a force to arrest Jesus, a collusion not mentioned in the synoptic gospels. There is no indication, however, that the Pharisees had any influence, let alone control, over either Roman soldiers or Temple guards at this time.

[19] John's narrative differs in this regard; here the high priests attempt to have Jesus arrested as early as John 7:32.

[20] Anthony J. Saldarini, "Pharisees," *ABD* (New York: Doubleday, 1992) 5:295–96.

itinerant preacher, was at the feast of Passover. At these celebrations the population of Jerusalem swelled by hundreds and thousands as Jews from throughout the Fertile Crescent and the Mediterranean Basin came on pilgrimage to celebrate the feast. Passover, you may recollect, was a celebration of God's liberation of the Hebrews enslaved in Egypt.[21] The similarity between their ancestors' servitude and their own subjection by Rome made these holidays a flashpoint for discontent. Josephus, for example, recounted how the Jews rioted after a disrespectful Roman soldier dropped his drawers while guarding the walls of the Temple at a Passover feast while Cumanus was procurator (48 C.E.). The Romans slaughtered twenty thousand Jews in quelling that disturbance.[22] The chief priests, who were placed in power by the Romans to keep order, were summarily replaced in these circumstances when they proved unable or unwilling to restrain their fellow Judeans' zeal for independence.

It is in that light that we should view the manner in which, according to Matthew, Mark, and Luke, Jesus, at the end of his ministry, entered Jerusalem in the overheated environment before Passover with crowds of rapturous followers chanting of "messianic hopes" and "David's coming kingdom." Level-headed Pharisees, understanding the possibly catastrophic consequences for everyone, not simply Jesus' followers, would have done well to encourage him to rein in the enthusiasm of his followers (Luke 19:39). Even an opponent might suggest that it could be detrimental to all to exhibit so blatantly an essentially anti-Roman sentiment. Jesus, though, proceeded directly to the Temple and assumed control over the purveyors of the unblemished animals on sale there as though, in fact, he *were* the messiah.[23] The chief priests would have immediately recognized Jesus as a threat to both civic order and their lofty yet precarious position. It is for this reason that they acted so quickly and decisively. The synoptic gospels depict Jesus' arrest, trial, public prosecution for political crimes before Pontius Pilate, and subsequent public execution following quickly thereafter.

Thus the hostilities between Jesus and the Pharisees only *seem* to build to a climax in Jesus' death but really are unrelated, since the Passion narratives clearly lay responsibility at the feet of the Temple authorities. In

---

[21] For a quick review of Israelite, Jewish, and early Christian history, and in particular the Exodus event and the Passover, see Barbara Green et al., *From Earth's Creation to John's Revelation*. Interfaces (Collegeville: Liturgical Press, 2003) 11–13.

[22] Josephus, *Ant.* 17.9.3; 20.5.3; *War* 2.1.3.

[23] Again John differs, depicting the "cleansing of the Temple" much earlier in his gospel (2:13-17).

light of this it has been reasonably suggested that the most hostile elements of the literary portrayal of the Pharisees in the gospel narrative of Jesus' life may have been a literary creation of the evangelists, both to assist the plot and to reflect their own later historical situation in which tensions between Pharisees and Christians had come to the fore.[24] That is not to say that Jesus didn't have encounters, and even strong disagreements, with Pharisees. Some of them, though, may reflect originally less hostile engagements in which the historical Jesus expressed divergence of belief from the historical (as opposed to narratively portrayed) Pharisees in the kind of lively, but hardly deadly, disagreements so commonly expressed in later Jewish literature such as the Mishnah. Considerable fierceness pervades its intramural rabbinic debates, although they were only occasionally personal and rarely threatening.[25] For a similar intramural Christian debate, even about comparable details of public associations and dining and with no less assertiveness, consider Paul's description of Peter's behavior in Antioch (Gal 2:11-14).

We have the frank confession of an ex-Pharisee, Paul, written roughly fifteen years before the composition of Mark's gospel, of how, in his former life, he harshly persecuted the church, aiming to destroy it, all the while progressing beyond his generation in his observance of Judaism, zealous for his ancestral traditions (Gal 1:13-14). It was this very zeal for the traditions that grounded Paul's persecution of the church. Curiously, though, none of Paul's letters, composed in the early to mid-fifties C.E., makes an issue of the Pharisees, for good or ill, or connect them to his activities.

The incorporation of anti-Pharisaic content only begins with Mark, the first of the gospels, written in the late sixties or early seventies C.E. By this time at least some early Christian communities had experienced difficulties with the Pharisees, even before the destruction of the Temple, when many scholars presume that the Pharisees achieved greater religious influence. Mark's explanation of Hebrew terminology (e.g., Mark 7:11) and Jewish ritual practices (e.g., Mark 7:1-4) for the sake of his audience suggests that they lived at some distance from Judea and were not personally acquainted with its internal politics and styles of religious debate. Mark may or may not have been a Jew himself. Even if he were, though, it would be easy for Mark (as well as the contemporary reader) to be confused by the aggressive tone of the debates between Jesus and his contemporary

---

[24] Saldarini, "Pharisees," 295.

[25] If the reader has never examined the Mishnah at any length, it might be useful to do so, even if only to read passages at random. Even a brief perusal will demonstrate the above point.

rabbis. Mark was, perhaps, inclined to give too much weight to the intensity of these debates. Thus a combination of the experience of rejection of Christianity by Pharisaic Judaism, and perhaps even persecution of early church members by devout Pharisees, such as was carried out by Paul in his earlier days, plus a misperception of intramural Jewish debates as engaged in by Jesus and his contemporary Pharisaic opponents, could easily have led Mark to mistake more innocent events during the life of Jesus for the pained conflicts of his own day.

As was discussed in Chapter One of this book, Mark's gospel, in both its content and arrangement, was used as the foundation for the gospels of Matthew and Luke. Writing between ten and twenty years after Mark, Matthew and Luke add traditions concerning the Pharisees from a source common to both of them. The way they shape the common traditions and their own unique material, however, differs. Luke's additions are made up of some negative portrayals, but also include some, such as Luke 7:36-50, that could be interpreted as either neutral or even positive in their perspective on individual Pharisees. Matthew's embellishments, on the other hand, are unrelentingly hostile. By way of comparison, where Matthew takes twenty-two verses to express four woes against the Pharisees (Matt 23:13-35), Luke includes only three, stating them in only three verses (Luke 11:42-44).

Both of the evangelists altered the tradition they received from Mark to include the Pharisees where they were not originally mentioned. We find this in Matt 9:32-34; 12:22-24; 22:34-40; Luke 5:17-26; 7:36-50. Each of these passages recounts incidents, paralleled in the other two synoptic gospels, in which they clarify that it was the Pharisees who opposed Jesus, though they were absent in Mark's earlier version. Where they both make such changes it might be claimed that they shared a common preexistent source, but these changes were not common to both Matthew and Luke in any of the above cases. Although they each could have had independent sources for these alterations, especially in the case of Matthew 9:32-34 and 12:22-24, which are redundant, it is still more likely, given the frequency with which this happened, that it reflected anti-Pharisaic editorial policies on the part of both Matthew and Luke.

What explains the additional, hostile material, common to Luke and Matthew? How do we explain Matthew's vituperative intensity? In addition to Christianity's rejection of the Pharisees' ancestral traditions, and the Pharisees' rejection of the Christian belief in the resurrection and in Jesus' relationship with the Father, the strained relationship between the two movements seems to have been exacerbated by the destruction of Jerusalem in 70 C.E.

Roughly concurrent with Mark's composition of the gospel or slightly thereafter, depending on how the evidence in Mark 13 is interpreted, the Romans responded to a Jewish rebellion by assailing and destroying Jerusalem. At that time the Romans toppled all the Judean religious and political institutions and destroyed the Temple itself. The destruction of the Temple reverberated throughout late-first-century Jewish consciousness. There was no longer a place for sacrifice, for celebrating the Passover, or for procuring the ashes of the red heifer, so necessary for the bathing rituals through which one obtained ritual purity. The priests and their Temple rites could no longer serve as the central focus of religious practice. If Judaism were to survive, it had to find a new center. The Sadducees, to whatever degree they were actually to be identified with either the priesthood or the leadership of the Temple and Jerusalem, no longer had either. They became functionless. The Essenes, to whatever degree their beliefs were reflected by the literature at Qumran, had eschatological expectations that involved their retaking the Temple and restoring proper worship there. The destruction of the Temple revealed their religious expectation as a fantasy.

There were, however, two movements, Pharisaism and Christianity, with visions for Judaism that incorporated much of what was so rich from the past, including a sense of election and an understanding of the ongoing commitment of God to the Jewish people, but did not necessitate the Temple. Paul, for one, had argued vehemently two decades before the Temple's destruction that the merits of Christ had obviated the need for the works of the Law, embodied in rites of sacrifice and ritual purity. It is argued by Jacob Neusner that the Pharisees took a different approach, pressing for the adoption of the religious practices of the priests in their maintenance of purity around the sacred, by the laity in their homes and, particularly, around their tables.[26]

Thus by the time the gospels were being written, the Pharisees and the early Christians had become, by virtue of their success at negotiating a religious world without a Temple, stiff competitors for the soul of Judaism. Both actively sought to determine, in the highly transitional post-Temple world, the way Judaism would define itself, emphasizing the importance of the daily life of the non-priest. It was inevitable that they would have contended with each other, and a certain amount of acrimony was to be expected as they competed for the affections of the general Jewish population, both in the Diaspora and in Judea and Galilee. Add to this Christianity's apocalyptic fervor, in which the Temple's destruction was a clear sign

---

[26] Neusner, *Purity in Rabbinic Judaism,* 109

of the world's immanent end. The result is that the early Christians were all the more earnest to convince the Jewish population of the correctness of Christian beliefs. They did this, in part, by rooting their disputes in controversies between Jesus and their opponents, the Pharisees.

The end result was that the authors of the New Testament were motivated by something other than historical authenticity. They had to respond to the early church's failed mission to Judaism and the consequences suffered by the Jewish Christians who were surely devastated by their exclusion from the synagogue and in many cases their alienation from their own families. Though it seems unlikely that the Pharisees were responsible for Jesus' death, they were portrayed as working toward that end from the beginning.

This evaluation of the polemical nature of the New Testament's portrayal of the Pharisees, and its roots in both difference of belief and historical circumstances, does not necessitate that we dismiss out of hand what the New Testament has to say. We will have to read its portrayal, though, with a conscious awareness of its limitations, since the outsider's perspective constrains the authors' understanding of Pharisees while the hostile, polemic tone suggests a lack of ordinary objectivity and approval, and the authors' use of them as literary devices further shades any element of strict historicity. We will find details of varying degrees of accuracy describing observable behavior and belief, but we will necessarily have many questions to ask of the material we do have.

Flavius Josephus

Flavius Josephus, literate in both Hebrew and Greek, and an active participant in the Jewish War, originally as a supposedly unenthusiastic rebel and later as prisoner and even a sycophant to the invading Romans, had much to accomplish in his literary works, no small portion of which was justifying his own behavior in switching sides.

Scholars note that Josephus was not consistent in his treatment of the Pharisees. Early on, he took a neutral tone toward them in *The Jewish War*, and he gave a seemingly more positive portrayal in his later book, *Antiquities of the Jews*. In both books he clearly aims to justify the behavior, beliefs, and lifestyle of his Jewish contemporaries to the Greco-Roman world, especially after the Jewish rebellion, during which Jews came to be looked upon with particular suspicion. Even before then both Greeks and Romans were suspicious of Jews for their perceived xenophobic withdrawal from public affairs. In a syncretistic age, when most people felt free to worship at the temples of Athena when in Athens, Artemis when in

Ephesus, and even Adonai (the Hebrew word for "LORD") when in Jerusalem, the Jews participated in no religious events other than their own. Since most civic events, including cultural offerings, began with invocation and offerings to the local gods, the absence of Jews was notable even outside the temples. They were known for not allowing their daughters to marry outside their ranks. Their failure to participate in public feasts, when the food served was usually first sacrificed or offered on the altars of the gods, and was not prepared according to the dictates of Torah, further alienated Jews from their contemporaries.

At least initially, Josephus began his defense of the Jews by attempting to show their beliefs as rational and reasonable, and their behavior as tragically misguided but not indicative of a general belligerence. Josephus did *not* confuse Judaism with the Pharisaic movement, counting the Pharisees among three influential movements, including the Sadducees and the Essenes, the last of which he seemed to prefer. This may suggest that Josephus had sectarian reasons for portraying the Pharisees in less than positive light in his earlier work, at least in comparison to the Essenes.

As a member of an elite priestly house, Josephus seems to have been motivated at first by an upper-crust suspicion of the Pharisees, since they were a "popular" movement admired by the common, uneducated classes. It may strike our twenty-first-century egalitarian sensibilities as odd to look down on the majority, but it was not at all uncommon in the Greco-Roman world for members of upper social strata to look upon on their "social inferiors" with disdain. The very words *hoi polloi,* derogative to this day, are simply the Greek words for "the many."

The situation seems to have changed by the time of Josephus' later great literary work, *The Antiquities of the Jews,* in which he seems to have developed a more positive attitude toward the Pharisees. By that time the Essenes seem to have largely disappeared, their center in Qumran having been destroyed by the Romans in 68 C.E., and the Pharisees, it is proposed, had come into their own. A common theory holds that by this time Josephus hoped the Romans would give the Pharisees authority to administer what remained of Palestine, and he reworked his earlier material to portray them in a more positive light.

The theories surrounding Josephus' motivations are not without detractors. In any case, between his social location and its accompanying prejudices, his need to justify his own questionable activities in the war, and his desire to defend and explain Judaism to his non-Jewish contemporaries, we have good reason to look upon his many comments on the Pharisees with a healthy suspicion. This is not to invalidate them, but to invite caution.

The Mishnah

It used to be quite common to hold that the Mishnah was, as a whole, the final product of the trajectory of Pharisaic thought, faithfully recording the teachings of earlier Pharisaic rabbis as they came to be recorded by the beginning of the third century C.E. Of late, noting how few of the great personages in the Mishnah are actually identified as Pharisees, and the significant passage of time between their having lived (some of them from well before the time of Jesus) and the recording of their teachings in final written form around 200 C.E., a much more cautious approach has become common in regard to the Mishnah's connection with the Pharisees. Curiously, the material presentation of them in Josephus and his statements about their key convictions and observances are by and large ignored by the authors of the Mishnah, who concentrate on other matters.[27] On the other hand, although the connection between the Mishnah and the Pharisees is not altogether certain, there is a clear correlation between the Mishnah's general subject matter and the New Testament's portrayal of the Pharisees: Sabbath observance, ritual purity, appropriate dining fellowship, Temple offerings, oaths, tithing, and ethics.[28]

For example, the Mishnah's authors, like the Pharisees as portrayed in the New Testament, were very concerned with questions of ritual purity, as is evidenced by the numerous works they produced on the three topics pertinent to the subject:

(1) sources of uncleanness: *Ohalot, Negaim, Niddah, Makhshirin, Zabim, Tebul Yom;*

(2) objects and substances susceptible to uncleanness: *Kelim, Tohorot, Uqsin;*

(3) modes of purification: *Parah, Miqvaot, Yadayim.*[29]

Their writings show a determination to understand and maintain purity even while demonstrating a clear pattern of accommodating the cult of purity to contemporary first- and second-century needs. A part of this, as we will discuss below, was the apparent appropriation of priestly responsibility, prerogatives, and restrictions, their sacred objects, and their food (Lev 22:3-9), over the personages, vessels, and food of the laity, an embryonic pattern discernible in the much earlier New Testament portrayal of the Pharisees (e.g., Mark 7:1-4).

---

[27] Neusner, *The Rabbinic Traditions,* 239.
[28] Ibid. 246.
[29] Neusner, *Purity in Rabbinic Judaism,* 40.

The Mishnah responded to the crucial question of what it was to be Jewish in the world without a Temple, without Jerusalem, and without a geographical heart. It may well have been the case that its authors adopted the Pharisaic response since it satisfied the cultural need of the Jewish community to carry on in their quest for holiness when that need was critically heightened by the catastrophic events of the day.[30] Their answer was, in Jacob Neusner's words, "that sanctity persists, indelibly, in Israel, the people, in its way of life, in its land, in its priesthood, in its food, in its mode of sustaining life, in its manner of procreating and so sustaining the nation."[31] In the absence of a holy city, a Temple, and cultic rites, the Pharisees had ready substitutes: the village, the home, and, most importantly, meals.

> The setting was holy. The actors were holy. And what, specifically, they did which had to be protected in holiness was eating. For when they ate their food at home, they ate it the way priests did in the Temple. And the way priests ate their food in the Temple, that is, the cultic rules and conditions observed in that setting, was like the way God ate his food in the Temple.[32]

Ordinary, heretofore non-sacral food, eaten at home, and apart from the special sacrificial moments associated with the Temple and its priests, approached in holiness the utmost holy offerings of grain, meat, and drink that had been consumed by the priests or burned at the altar.

The secondary implications of such a stance were staggering, affecting the whole of human life, as Neusner indicates:

> First, all food, not only that for the altar, was to be protected in a state of levitical cleanness, thus holiness, that is, separateness. Second, the place in the Land in which the food was grown and kept was to be kept cultically clean, holy, just like the Temple. Third, the people, Israel, who were to eat that food were holy, just like the priesthood, in rank behind the Temple's chief caste. Fourth, the act of eating food anywhere in the Holy Land was analogous to the act of eating food in the temple, by the altar.[33]

---

[30] The Talmud explains the change this way: "The priests preserved their status by not passing on to everyone the rules of purity," but after the Temple's destruction "purity spread" among the laity as well. See *b. Bekh.* 30b; *y. Shab.* 1:3.

[31] Neusner, *Purity in Rabbinic Judaism,* 38.

[32] Ibid. 109.

[33] Jacob Neusner, *Judaic Law from Jesus to the Mishnah: A Systematic Reply to Professor E. P. Sanders* (Atlanta: Scholars, 1993) 27–28.

This message was in no way a radical departure from Torah.[34] In essence it was the ultimate victory of the Holiness Code, that is, the traditions found in Leviticus 18–26, with its insistence that all the land and its inhabitants were to be preserved in holiness, over the preoccupation with the Temple and city of Jerusalem found in the rest of the book of Leviticus.[35] The consequences of this shift should not be underplayed. Once purity rituals could be observed at home, neither Temple nor priesthood was essential.[36] The Temple's destruction in 70, while tragic, enabled the Pharisees and others of like mind to continue and even amplify their implementation of a household-based piety in the vacuum.

The process of laicizing the cult of purity began long before the destruction of the Temple, and even as early as 200 B.C.E.[37] It is easy to place the question in Mark 7:5, "Why do your disciples . . . eat with hands defiled?" in this context. We do not need to presume the finality and intensity of the final version of *m. Yadayim* in 70 C.E. Pharisaic practice to recognize that the question of washing hands was very much a part of the process of determining how the laity would apply the Torah's instruction on eating sacred food. In fact, the very concentrated focus of *m. Yadayim* on the manner in which and the reasons for which hands were to be cleansed indicates a long period of reflection, application, and challenge.

In spite of this similarity between the small evidence in the New Testament and its correspondence with the broad sweep of Mishnaic content, Neusner reports that the Mishnah only rarely refers to Pharisees. Furthermore, only a few of the Mishnah's authorities, particularly Gamaliel and Simeon ben Gamaliel, have independent attestation as members of the Pharisaic movement by Paul and Josephus. As a result, writes Neusner, "to assign the whole of the Mishnah to the Pharisees who flourished before A.D. 70 and who are known to us from diverse sources, all of them composed in the form in which we know them after A.D. 70, is hardly justified."[38] So, for example, the earliest record we have to identify Hillel and

[34] Hannah K. Harrington, *The Impurity Systems of Qumran and the Rabbis* (Atlanta: Scholars, 1993) 63.

[35] Jacob Milgrom, "The Laws of Purity of the Temple Scroll," in Lawrence H. Schiffman, ed., *Archaeology and History in the Dead Sea Scrolls* (Sheffield: JSOT Press, 1990) 86–89.

[36] Neusner has concluded from his meticulously detailed study of rabbinical traditions about the Pharisees that of the 341 individual rulings from first-century Judaism, no fewer than 229 directly or indirectly pertain to table fellowship, approximately 67% of the whole (Neusner, *Rabbinic Traditions*, 97).

[37] Roger P. Booth, *Jesus and the Laws of Purity: Tradition History and Legal History in Mark 7* (Sheffield: JSOT Press, 1986) 131.

[38] Jacob Neusner, *The Mishnah: A New Translation* (New Haven: Yale University Press, 1988) xxxii–xxxiii.

Shammai as Pharisees is Jerome's fifth-century commentary, almost half a millennium after their lives. Since much of what we know about their lives was contained in the Mishnah, completed over a century after this time of consolidation, as opposed to their own more divisive and contentious times, any identification of them as Pharisees, if they were indeed such, would no longer have been pertinent. By the time of the Mishnah their earlier discussions played a significant part in defining mainstream Judaism.

Second, any equation of the world of the Mishnah with the world of first-century Judaism is problematic. E. P. Sanders suggests that the Mishnah did not entirely and accurately describe Jewish religious life in the Second Temple Period, even when it specifically sought to do so, claiming that some of the Mishnaic material, as regards Temple sacrifice, was actually second-century invention.[39] His caution is well advised. There were simply too many years and too many significant events between the first century and the composition of the Mishnah at the end of the second century to allow us to assume exact equivalency between Pharisaic positions and the ideas and beliefs expressed in the Mishnah. Most importantly as regards cultural analysis, the destruction of the Temple, the primary focus of Jewish cultic life, in 70 C.E., and the deportation of Jews from Judea as a result of the Bar Kokhba revolt of 132–135 C.E., will have had a *profound* impact on the practice of Jewish religiosity. Two of the three foci for the purity legislation of both Torah and the sects, that is, the Temple and the land, were destroyed or taken away from the third focus, that is, the people.

As a result of the destruction of the Temple, Jews were faced with at least three difficult choices: (1) abandon the laws as purposeless without the Temple and the Land, (2) maintain the cultic rules in a hopeless conviction that they could regain their homeland and rebuild the Temple, or (3) give their older Temple- and Land-based religious observances substantially new rationales, based on the importance of the purity of the people rather than the Land or the Temple. Wherever Jews took the first approach they effectively ceased to be Jews and were most likely assimilated into the other religious and cultural frameworks of the day. Those who chose the second option were faced with impossible requirements to maintain purity and observe sacrifices that simply could not be accomplished without a holy city, without a Temple and its sacrifices. This choice was no more than a delay before the inevitable selection of one of the two other options. The third option, I hold, was in fact exercised by those who refashioned Judaism into what we know today as Rabbinic Judaism.

---

[39] E. P. Sanders, *Judaism: Practice and Belief 63 B.C.E.–66 C.E.* (Philadelphia: Trinity Press International, 1990) 11, 103–104.

They accomplished this by making use of the program, most likely already initiated in Pharisaic Judaism before the destruction of the Temple, of borrowing the observance of purity from the Temple and the priests and applying it toward the sanctification of the home and the layperson. We can see evidence of such a practice in the extension of the priestly obligation to be ritually clean before eating the sacred portions (Lev 22:1-7) in a ritually clean place (Lev 10:14) to the Pharisaic "tradition of the ancestors" that required laypersons to wash hands before they ate and to maintain their homes in purity (Mark 7:1-5). Originally the sanctified home was intended as a complement and not a replacement for the Temple in the earliest manifestations of the Pharisaic movement. Only with time would there have been a sufficient development of thought and ritual that it could serve to replace the Temple.

The Political and Religious Influence of the Pharisees

There are hints in the New Testament and Josephus that Pharisaism provided many people with an uplifting religious experience. It is necessary, though, to read thoughtfully between the lines of the New Testament, focusing less on its polemic content than on the peripheral substance of the discussions to detect hints of a credible religious movement. For example, the Pharisees appear everywhere in the gospels: in Galilee and in Judea, in the countryside, in small towns and in the capital city of Jerusalem.[40] This wide geographical spread suggests that the Pharisees were not simply a "local" movement, but one that had experienced success among both country folk and city dwellers from all the large pools of Jewish population in the Levant. This coincides with the New Testament admission that the Pharisees had some success at recruiting disciples (Mark 2:18//Luke 5:33), apparently going to great efforts to make converts (Matt 23:15). As part of their educational strategy some of them became proficient teachers of the Pharisaic position on the Law, such as Gamaliel, who was "held in honor by all the people" (Acts 5:34), and this in spite of the overall hostile tone of the New Testament.

Josephus also attests to this, contrasting the high level of esteem the Pharisees received from the masses to the relatively unpopular Sadducees,

---

[40] Galilee: Mark 2:13-16; Luke 5:17; Judea: Matt 19:1-3; Mark 10:1-2; Luke 5:17; John 4:1-3; a field: Mark 2:23-24; a village: Luke 17:12-20; Jerusalem: Matt 15:1; Luke 5:17; John 2:23–3:1; 11:55-57; the Temple: Matt 21:45. See also Etienne Trocmé, *The Formation of the Gospel According to Mark,* trans. Pamela Gaughan (Philadelphia: Westminster, 1975) 53, n. 1.

who could only garner support from the affluent in Jerusalem (*Ant.* 13.10.6). Their influence over the populace, in fact, was so great, wrote Josephus, that the Pharisees were believed even while speaking out against the king or high priest (*Ant.* 13.288). Living in a more egalitarian age, it is important that we consider whether Josephus was complimenting the Pharisees or not in this regard. Josephus, as a member of the upper crust of Judean society, writing for others of the same social class, may not have intended a description of popularity among the populace as flattering. Adulation from the "great unwashed," the ignorant who know no better, was not something to which Josephus and his social class could admit an aspiration. The implication seems to be that the Pharisees were only one step above the peasants among whom they were most popular.

Their popularity should not be understood to imply control or dominance. Any sense of a monolithic Judaism at the time of Jesus, led by Pharisaic rabbis, should be discarded. There is abundant evidence that the Pharisees were neither the only nor the chief religious movement of Judaism while Jesus was alive. The range of Jewish expression during the first century appears to have been broad, with interest groups active among Jews, with varying degrees of influence, in Palestine and the Diaspora reflecting a wide variety of perspectives. The leading council in Jerusalem, the Sanhedrin, was made up of members from an assortment of groups, including chief priests, scribes, elders, Sadducees, and Pharisees (Acts 5:34; 23:1-9). In addition to these we can also include Essenes, Boethusians, Josephus' Fourth Philosophy, various other politically motivated bands of anti-Roman revolutionaries, and other religious and civic groups that passed into and out of existence without leaving literary traces for us.

Though John once depicts the Pharisees arguing among themselves (John 9:16), the New Testament most often portrays the Pharisees in cooperative groups, even if it is only to highlight how they collaborated in opposing Jesus. Josephus wrote that they were respectful of their elders and careful not to contradict them (*Ant.* 18.12), that they had an amiable spirit among themselves and were on harmonious terms with the general populace (*War* 2.166).[41] In this same spirit the Pharisees entered into cooperative relationships with members of some of the other groups operating around them at the time. Both Josephus and the New Testament demonstrate temporary partnerships between Pharisees and the chief priests: In *Life* 21 Josephus, reporting on his own attempts to head off the revolt against Rome that led to the destruction of Judea, says he met with the chief priests and the leading Pharisees. Again, the Pharisee Simon ben

---

[41] See n. 17 above.

Gamaliel convinced a Sadducean high priest, Ananus, to send three Pharisees and another man to remove Josephus from office.[42] In Matthew's and John's gospels the chief priests and Pharisees regularly cooperate in joint ventures.[43]

We can perceive a consistent, active engagement in the religious and political life of Judea, though while the Pharisees were apparently successful with the former, they were not so with the latter. Virtually all the Pharisees depicted in Josephus and some of those in the New Testament were politically involved.[44] Nicodemus was one of the chief rulers of the Jews (John 3:1). Gamaliel was a participant in the Sanhedrin (Acts 5:34). Saddock was one of the cofounders of Josephus' Fourth Philosophy, a movement crushed by the Romans (*Ant.* 18.4). Even Josephus, a self-identified Pharisee at least during his youth, was a political opportunist, a supposedly reluctant revolutionary leader, and a Roman quisling, all in turn. Although as a group Pharisees initially had passing favor with John Hyrcanus, the king and high priest (134–104 B.C.E.), for being righteous and desiring to please God, unfortunate circumstances, apparently not of their devising, lost them royal favor. When Eleazar, a person of uncertain allegiance who seems not to have been a Pharisee, grievously offended John Hyrcanus, he asked the Pharisees for an appropriate punishment. They, unfortunately, did not propose execution and suffered lasting political harm (*Ant.* 13.288-298). At about this time the Pharisees achieved their only real, be it ever so brief, political influence. Josephus describes at length how they took advantage of the trust placed in them by Queen Alexandra during the nine years of her reign (76 to 67 B.C.E.). As the queen's public administrators they banished or removed from office, executing important public figures as they saw fit. Their poor behavior aggravated Aristobulus, Alexandra's younger son, so greatly that he seized the throne belonging properly to his older brother, Hyrcanus.[45] This period does not reflect well on the Pharisees. From that point on Josephus portrays a marked hostility between the Pharisees and the Hasmoneans.[46] Thus Mark's description of the Pharisees and the Herodians conspiring to put Jesus to death simply does not have the semblance of historicity to it (Mark 3:6). The Pharisees' influence over the common folk never seems to obtain for them access to lasting political power.

---

[42] *Life* 191–332a; *War* 2.627-631.

[43] Matt 21:45-46; 27:62; John 7:32, 45; 11:47, 57; 18:3.

[44] Sievers, "Who Were the Pharisees?" 153.

[45] *War* 1.110-114; *Ant.* 13.398-432.

[46] Only Pollion, a contemporary of Herod the Great, comes away with political favor, although no apparent influence (*Ant.* 14.172-176; 15.3-4).

Asceticism and Wealth

Luke claims that Pharisees were money-loving (Luke 16:14); however, the gospels never portray the Pharisees in any moneymaking activity, whereas Josephus gives a few examples. In the first, Herod accused the wife of Pheroras of giving money to the Pharisees as a reward for carrying out unmentioned activities opposing him (*War* 1.571). Evaluating this episode is difficult since Herod was known for his obsessive paranoia, and thus the accusation may have had no grounds. Furthermore, there were many legitimate reasons, both political and moral, for the Pharisees to oppose Herod the Great, which may even have involved the innocent exchange of money. Josephus recounts another episode in which individual Pharisees bribed the high priest to achieve unjust ends which, though a considerably unsavory act, does not suggest too close an attachment to wealth (*Life* 195–203). Most damning, Josephus claims that they fabricated prophecies for monetary reasons, causing the ruin of those who trusted them.[47] Josephus offers contrary evidence, however, stating that as a general principle Pharisees did not espouse luxury, but led simple lives (*Ant.* 18.12). In support of this and, oddly, in Luke's gospel as well, the proud Pharisee praying in the Temple, while admittedly filled with hubris, proclaimed his rejection of greed and dishonesty and asserted that he paid tithes on his entire income (Luke 18:10-14). Among the points that should be noted here is that not all the portrayals of the Pharisees in either Josephus or the New Testament, and even in the same book in the New Testament, are consistent with each other.

What should we conclude from the evidence? Luke's general statement of the Pharisees' love of money is both countered and supported by evidence in his own text, and by Josephus as well. It is reasonable that at least *some* Pharisees could have been unduly interested in money, and yet others, maybe even the majority, were admirably ascetic. Even the most austere religious movements can have members that exhibit "acquisitive" behaviors in contradiction to their stated religious values. This question may not be resolvable in a clear black and white fashion, but we should expect this kind of ambiguity whenever we allow for the full range of human behavior. Was there ever a religious movement in which all the members faithfully lived out their stated values?

---

[47] Josephus recounts how the populace believed that Pharisees had foreknowledge through divine inspiration. At the same time, though, his narrative suggests they were frauds in that their predictions led to disastrous consequences for their own numbers and for others (*Ant.* 17.41-45).

Fidelity to the Law

As regards the observance of the Law, if we temporarily set aside any moral evaluation of legalism and hypocrisy we find a lay association, dedicated to conforming itself to God's law, as they understood it, according to the strictest observance. In this regard the gospels and Paul both seem to view the Pharisees as embodying fidelity to Jewish law (Phil 3:5; Acts 26:5). They appealed to the Mosaic Law when permitting divorce.[48] Even Matthew admitted that, because the Pharisees had the chair of Moses, their teachings were to be observed, if not their behavior (Matt 23:1-3). As noted above, Jesus, in both Matthew and Luke, comments that they were *correct* to observe their tithes on herbs (Luke 11:42//Matt 23:23).

Pharisees believed that those who did not know the Law were accursed (John 7:49). It was precisely their insistence on a full living out of the commandments of the Law, again as they understood it, and Jesus' failure to observe the Pharisaic interpretation that brought them into conflict with him. This was particularly the case in reference to working on the Sabbath,[49] but also to lesser degrees regarding hand-washing (Mark 7:5) and Jesus' companionship with tax collectors and public sinners.[50]

Even in the manner in which they investigated infractions of the Law their activities were guided by laws requiring two witnesses for testimony against defendants, and outside verification whenever the accused gave testimony on their own behalf.[51] We can detect their strict interpretation of punishments in their approval of stoning adulterers (John 8:3-5) and putting to death those who failed in their observance of the Sabbath rest.[52] Notably, they also felt empowered to pursue and prosecute notable offenders.[53] Josephus had a more tempered view of the New Testament's fairly persistent portrayal of their willingness to execute lawbreakers, describing them as disinclined to severity (*Ant.* 13.294) and even providing examples of their clemency, as in the case of Eleazar above (p. 62).

The New Testament at times portrays the Pharisees participating in religious devotions, for example, circumcising infants on the eighth day (Phil 3:5), and expressly calling for circumcision for adult male converts in accordance with the law of Moses (Acts 15:4-6). Pharisees prayed in the Temple (Luke 5:33; 18:10-12) and were noted for fasting with some fre-

---

[48] Mark 10:2-4; Matt 19:3-8; see Deut 24:1-4.

[49] Mark 2:24//Matt 12:2//Luke 6:2; Luke 14:1-6; John 9:13-16.

[50] Matt 9:10-12//Mark 2:15-17//Luke 5:30-32.

[51] John 8:13, 17; Deut 17:6; 19:15; Num 35:30.

[52] Mark 2:24//Matt 12:2//Luke 6:2; Luke 14:1-6; John 9:13-16; see Exod 31:14-15.

[53] Mark 3:6//Matt 12:14//Luke 6:11.

quency.[54] Josephus wrote more than once that that Pharisees "appeared" more religious than others and more precise in their interpretation of the Law.[55] Even if Josephus' phraseology suggests that he may not have agreed with the majority perception, it is still important to recognize the popular opinion.[56]

The Tradition of the Elders

One cannot help but notice, however, that there were elements of Pharisaic observance, at least as described in the New Testament, that were not based on the Torah, strictly understood as the Pentateuch, the first five books of the Hebrew Bible: Genesis, Exodus, Leviticus, Numbers, and Deuteronomy.[57] As alluded to by Mark 7:5, and verified by both Josephus and the Mishnah, the Pharisees had passed on an ancestral tradition, in addition to the content of Torah, by which they regulated themselves.[58] The Pharisees believed that Moses received this tradition at Sinai, and that it was handed down in oral fashion along with the written Torah, with which it shared an equal authority. Some, maybe even most scholars suggest that this tradition, in large part, took written form in the Mishnah.[59] This ancestral tradition surfaces in the New Testament when the Pharisees question Jesus concerning the failure of his disciples to wash their hands before eating (Mark 7:5//Matt 15:1-2). As Jesus will point out, there is no general requirement in Torah for the washing of hands. There is, furthermore, conflicting evidence concerning the observance of *qorban* vows, another supposedly Pharisaic practice to which Jesus objects (Mark 7:6-13//Matt 15:3-11).

---

[54] Mark 2:18//Matt 9:14//Luke 5:33; Luke 18:12.

[55] *War* 1.110; 2.162; *Life* 1.191.

[56] However, when Josephus speaks of "the law," while it would be easy to presume that he refers specifically to the five books of the Pentateuch, a careful reading of his texts suggests otherwise. Josephus' various uses of legal terminology, scattered throughout his texts, often deviate from what we know of the requirements of Torah, incorporating extra-biblical material. See Mason, *Flavius Josephus on the Pharisees*, 98–100.

[57] "Torah," though very commonly translated as "the law," more properly means "instruction" in Hebrew. "Pentateuch," on the other hand, is a Greek word meaning "a work with five books."

[58] Mark 7:3-4; *Ant.* 13.297-298; *m. Peah* 2:6; *m. Eduy.* 8:7; *Abot* 1:1; Lawrence H. Schiffman, *Sectarian Law in the Dead Sea Scrolls: Courts, Testimony and the Penal Code* (Chico, CA: Scholars, 1983) 16.

[59] Frederick J. Murphy, *The Religious World of Jesus: An Introduction to Second Temple Palestinian Judaism* (Nashville: Abingdon, 1991) 221.

This same inclusion of non-Torah-based legislation is found in the Mishnah. Neusner claims that the Mishnah's authors selectively borrowed some material straight from the Hebrew Bible, sometimes with only logical expansions, but according to what was in accord with their own criterion of interest.[60] At other times they began with the contents of the Scriptures but diverged from the biblical authors' intent, creatively adapting the Scriptures, making logical leaps and drawing conclusions beyond the initial scope of biblical materials.[61] They also, however, expounded on issues found nowhere or only obliquely in the Bible.[62] In effect, while the authors of the Mishnah were unreserved in their affirmation of scriptural authority, in practice they were selective both in choice and application of scriptural content.[63] One cannot help but wonder if this Mishnaic approach to law was founded on the earlier Pharisaic manner of legal adaptation and interpretation or was simply the acceptable standard of the day.

The Pharisees' non-Pentateuch-based beliefs appear to have been handed down in an oral tradition from their elders (Mark 7:3, 5; Matt 15:2). This body of beliefs receives wide attestation, having been mentioned by Paul in Acts, by Pharisees in the gospels, and about Pharisees by Josephus, who wrote of their many observances, not included in the law of Moses but received from their fathers, which the Pharisees conveyed to the people and by which the multitude were apparently persuaded.[64] Unfortunately he speaks of this tradition in only the broadest terms, largely neglecting the

---

[60] Neusner, *Judaic Law,* 20–21.

[61] E.g., *m. Parah's* treatment of the burning of the red heifer differed from the Scriptures in its understanding of the absolute purity required for a time and place that the priestly author of Numbers viewed, essentially, as unclean. *M. Erubin* and *m. Besah* took similar contrastive positions to the Hebrew Bible. John Corbett makes this point in blunter fashion concerning the oral law of the Pharisees, stating, "If we accept that the oral law was derived, as we would say, from the written Law by new techniques of exegesis, especially citing of proof texts 'out of context,' we can recognize how the oral Law could be as revolutionary as the sources indicate while still being closely associated with the written Law in which it was surely considered by the Pharisees to be implicit" (John Corbett, "The Pharisaic Revolution and Jesus as Embodied Torah," *SR* 15 [1986] 377).

[62] E.g., *Tohorot* and *Uqsin* on the cleanness of foods; *Demai* on doubtfully tithed produce; *Tamid* on the conduct of the daily whole-offering; *Baba Batra* on real estate transactions and other business concerns; *Ohalot* on the unique comparison of vessels and tents; *Kelim* on the susceptibility of various types of utensils to uncleanness; and *Miqvaot* on the types of water effective for purification from uncleanness. For another approach to the development of Mishnaic thought and writings see Neusner, *Judaic Law,* 26–46.

[63] Bruce Chilton and Jacob Neusner, *Judaism in the New Testament: Practices and Beliefs* (New York: Routledge, 1995) 24–31.

[64] Gal 1:13-14; Acts 28:17; Mark 7:5; *Ant.* 13.10.6, 297-298, 408; 17.41.

actual content of this belief. He may give us a clue, though, as to how they arrived at this tradition when he wrote that they do "what [reason] prescribes to them as good for them . . . and they think that they sought earnestly to strive to observe reason's dictates for practice" (*Ant.* 18.1.3).

How Pharisees related the tradition of the ancestors to the Mosaic Law is not deliberately clarified by either Josephus or the New Testament. The Christian perspective, voiced by Jesus, was, of course, to reject this tradition altogether as a human invention (Mark 7:6-9//Matt 15:3-9). It goes without saying that the Pharisees did not view it that way. Serious scholars of the development of the Mishnah, when juxtaposing what the Torah actually *does* say on matters such as washing and vows with the expressed beliefs of the Pharisees in the New Testament, and then finally tracing the trajectory to its expression in the Mishnah, are able to hypothesize convincingly on the likely "Pharisaic agenda," so to speak.

As mentioned earlier, the Pharisees in the New Testament encouraged Jews to wash their hands before eating, especially after coming from the marketplace (Mark 7:1-5//Matt 15:1-2). They also ritually cleansed jugs, cups, dishes, and pots (Mark 7:4; Matt 23:25//Luke 11:39). The Mishnah, too, has an entire book, *m. Yadayim,* dedicated to discussions of the manner in which hands are both defiled and washed. The actual dictates of Torah, however, are much less detailed, in fact only pertaining to priests and their families, and only to the extent that they were to eat their Temple portions from the sacrifices while ritually pure and in a pure place. This, of course, presumes that both had been maintained as ritually pure through ablutions of some kind. Their "portion," that is, the food set aside for them, their sons, and sometimes their entire families, was sacred, having been offered as a sacrifice on the altar to God by worshipers as cereal offerings, sin offerings, guilt offerings, and the raised and waved offerings. It was precisely to maintain this sacredness or to prevent profaning these offerings that both priests and their family members were obliged to eat their share of the offerings while in a state of ritual purity, and in a sacred place.[65] Such cleanliness of person and place would, if actually observed, inevitably have led to stringent and daily bathing before dining on the priestly households offerings. No such obligation is laid upon the laity by Torah when eating ordinary food.

Some scholars suggest, relying in large part on Mark 7 and Matthew 15, that the Pharisaic reform attempted to apply the practices associated with the lives of the priests and their worship in the Temple to the daily

---

[65] Lev 6:9-11, 18-19; 7:6-10; 10:12-15; 22:1-16; Num 18:11; Ezek 42:13.

lives and homes of the Jews. Thus, as the priests were to maintain the sanctity and purity of the Temple and its altar, so the homes, tables, and dining utensils of Jews should be kept free from ritual defilement. Just as the priests and their families were to bathe their bodies as necessary before consuming their sacred portions in a ritually clean place, all Jews should bathe their bodies, and especially their hands, lest they inadvertently spread the contagion of defilement. According to Mark 7, the rationale of the ancestral tradition was that people, and in particular their hands, could become ritually unclean or defiled in the marketplace. This uncleanness, in turn, could be passed on by touch to the food one consumed (Mark 7:1-5, 14-19). Ceremonial or cultic cleanness, differing from hygienic cleanness, could be restored by ritually washing in water. It was particularly important to do this before eating since, as both Mark's and Matthew's gospels indicate, Pharisees believed food, made unclean by being touched with unclean hands, in turn more thoroughly defiled the person who consumed it.[66] A further logical conclusion, implicit in this, is that they held that an individual's hands could be unclean while the person remained substantially, ritually pure, a curious distinction.

The Mishnah, however, agreeing with Jesus, states that unwashed hands do *not* defile common food (*m. Parah* 11:5). If the Mishnah is, in fact, a product of Pharisaic thought, or the end product of the trajectory of Pharisaic thought over a century later, this difference of teaching is somewhat striking. It is possible that Mark was simply mistaken in his portrayal of Pharisaic belief, and that Matthew copied his error. It is also possible that some Pharisees washed before dining and others did not. Finally, it is also within the realm of possibility that a practice, or interpretation of a practice, common among Pharisees of the first century died out before the composition of the Mishnah, finalized some time in the vicinity of 200 C.E.

Earlier archaeological evidence of the construction of cisterns for the purpose of ritual cleansing grants credence to the antiquity of concern for ritual bathing. E. P. Sanders points out that it was imperative that the water for such cleansing be living water, that is, from a flowing body of water (Lev 15:13).[67] In an arid climate such as Palestine this required the construction of not one, but two cisterns so that rain water gathered in the first storage cistern (*'ôtsar*) could be run through channels into the second cistern or bathing pool (*miqvah*). Only a small amount of drawn water, carried by buckets or such means, could be added to the storage cistern before

---

[66] Mark 7:4, 3-20; Matt 15:2, 11, 17-20; Luke 11:38.

[67] See also Num 19:17: For anyone who is thus unclean, ashes from the sin offering shall be put in a vessel, and spring water shall be poured on them.

it was no longer suited for purification purposes.[68] Sanders makes good use of archaeological evidence to show, curiously, that this practice was not observed by the priests of the Temple, by the aristocracy, or by the bulk of the populace. However, a fair number of the small homes of the lower classes of Jerusalem, which Sanders presumes, from Mishnaic evidence, belonged to Pharisees, contain both pools and a connecting channel.[69]

In a time when Jews had largely lost control over their own political destiny and were asking themselves how the Roman occupation was possible, it was inevitable that some would conclude, following the patterns of earlier prophetic warnings and exiles, that they had, as a nation, alienated their LORD God. Different segments of society would react to this issue in differing ways, ranging from defending the *status quo* to creative religious innovation. The Sadducees and chief priests, though dependent on the Romans, were in a position of power and perhaps the least motivated to change. They do not seem to have profoundly impacted the religious world except as regards the Temple. The Dead Sea Scrolls indicate that the Essenes called for a reform of priestly and Temple life, the restoration of the Zadokite family to the high priesthood, the reimplementation of an earlier religious calendar, and the return to what they understood to be a more authentic religious expression of Judaism. The Essenes appear to have failed in their quest, living on the margins of society or withdrawing altogether into quasi-monastic enclaves, and foreswearing the rest of Judaism.

The Pharisees, though, seemed to have provided the most innovative and successful strategy, which was the extension of Temple sanctity and priestly practice over the everyday lives of ordinary people. Such an interpretation fits the few Pharisaic practices we have detailed as well as other Pharisaic behaviors, readily evidenced throughout the New Testament, in which their leaders maintained the importance of public religiosity and ritual purity in the small town, in the city, or even in the field. In essence they called for a religious reform of all society. Rather than withdraw into the Temple or secede from public life, the Pharisees were actively engaged with their fellow Jews and inclined, with missionary zeal, to encourage society's participation in a common project of sanctifying the nation.[70] It was this very dedication to society that ultimately led them, even before the destruction of the Temple and long before the Mishnah's composition, to concern themselves in lively debates about how to achieve their social

---

[68] Only between .09 and 10.8 liters could be added to a pool that contained thousands of liters. *Eduyot* 1.3.

[69] *M. Miq.* 6.8; Sanders, *Practice and Belief,* 224–29.

[70] Harrington, *Impurity Systems of Qumran,* 58.

ends. With such a program it was inevitable that they would question and even object to Jesus who, as a religious leader, proved inattentive to ritual purity, dined regularly with sinners, participated in healing activities on the Sabbath, and whose disciples ate without washing their hands.[71]

It should be noted that in Mark 7//Matthew 15 the Pharisees ask Jesus about his disciples' lack of ritual cleansing before eating, but do not contest his rejoinder. Such silence here and elsewhere may indicate an unsettledness in the Pharisaic program, that religious opinion was still in flux and open to debate. It is significant that Jesus contests the practice on the very principle that it is not required, at least of ordinary people, by the Mosaic Law. Thus Jesus judged this innovative reform, which he calls "your tradition that you handed on" (Mark 7:8-9, 13), to be a "human tradition" rather than a legitimate interpretation of the Mosaic tradition of the Law. For Jesus the "ancestral traditions" of the Pharisees were not binding.

Another example in which the written law of Moses differed from the ancestral law regards care of parents and vows made to the contrary. The Torah is clear about the honor due one's parents (Exod 20:12; Deut 5:16). This precept appears to conflict with the Pharisaic interpretation of the *qorban* vow expressed in their ancestral tradition, restricting the use of possessions for a certain purpose. Originally, in the Hebrew Bible, the term *qorban* indicated that property had been dedicated to God as an offering or oblation.[72] Josephus noted the practice and even called it by the same name, *qorban*, using the same explanatory phrase found in a Markan aside in 7:11, "that is, 'gift.'"[73] He did not, however, relate this practice to the Pharisees. This sense of *qorban* as "offering" seems to be verified by archaeological remains. Joseph Fitzmyer describes an ossuary lid, found in a Jewish burial site at Jebel Hellet et-Turi, in southeast Jerusalem, dated around the first century and marked with the following message: "All that a man may find to his profit in this ossuary is an offering *(qorban)* to God from him who is within it."[74]

A secondary and perhaps originally unintended result of such vows was that it made the gifted property unavailable for other uses, for example,

---

[71] In response, when Q's Jesus was determined to challenge the hypocrisy he perceived in the Pharisaic movement he did so in the strongest, and almost certainly ironic, language of cultic defilement, referring to them as whitened sepulchers, filled with every sort of corruption.

[72] It is used in this fashion 82 times in the Hebrew Scriptures in four books, Leviticus, Numbers, Nehemiah, and Ezekiel, but is found in no other books. Compare with Matt 27:6, where the transliteration in Greek from the Hebrew *korbanan* refers to the Temple treasury.

[73] *Ant.* 4.73; *Apion* 1.167.

[74] Joseph A. Fitzmyer, "The Aramaic *Korban* Inscription from Jebel Hallet Et-Turi and Mark 7:11/Mt 15:5," *JBL* 78 (1959) 60–65.

as a means of support for parents. These vows seem to have taken on a more argumentative tenor when, in fits of pique, children made vows that, "by the Temple," their parents would not be receiving any assistance from them in their dotage.[75] Philo described such oaths, saying: "But there are some who, either because through excessive moroseness their nature has lost the sense of companionship and fellow-feeling or because they are constrained by anger which rules them like a stern mistress, confirm the savagery of their temper with an oath. They declare that they will not admit such and such a person to their board or under their roof, or again, that they will not render assistance to so and so or accept anything from him till his life's end. Sometimes they carry on their vindictiveness after that end has come and leave directions in their wills against even granting the customary rites to his corpse." Jesus' statement in Mark 7:8-13 suits this interpretation, for he accuses the Pharisees of setting their ancestral tradition above the law of God when they insist that such vows prevented the observance of the express command to honor, and thus provide for one's parents.[76]

The Mishnah was, of course, written at a time when it was no longer possible to give offerings to the Temple, which had been destroyed for over a century. Even so, it, too, refers to *qorban* vows (*m. Ned.* 63b) in which the property was reserved for God and no longer available for other certain stated purposes,[77] and also suggests anger as a common reason for binding oneself in such a drastic fashion (*m. Ned.* 5:6g). Curiously, the Mishnah agrees with Jesus and rebukes the practice for abandoning the more important command to care for parents for the sake of a vow. This is a curious about-face, if the scholars who trace the Mishnah's origins to the Pharisees are correct.

The following conclusions can be drawn from this study of *qorban*. The convergence of data from Mark, Philo, Josephus, and the Mishnah indicates that the observance of *qorban* vows with parents and others was a widespread custom, probably not limited to the Pharisees. The criticism of the practice by both Mark's and Matthew's Jesus, the Mishnah, and Philo indicates that such vows did not receive universal affirmation. Other Jews besides the early Christians were uncomfortable with the practice of vowing to permanently withhold property and care from parents, precisely because of the command to honor them. Had they been given the opportunity, the Pharisees might well have responded that they were simply allowing

---

[75] See Philo, *Special Laws* 2.16. Philo also knew of the practice of dedicating property to the Temple (*Hypothetica* 7.3-5).

[76] Also Matt 15:3-6; see Exod 20:12; Deut 5:16.

[77] *M. Ned.* 1:2a, 3e, 4h; 2:2a, 5bc; 3:2h, 5.

one dictate of the Law, on the importance of fulfilling vows without delay (Deut 23:21-23; Num 30:2-3), to supersede another, on appropriate behavior toward parents. The counterevidence from the Mishnah, however, may suggest that after the time of Jesus the Pharisees had a radical change of heart on *qorban* vows. It is also possible that Jesus' accusation against them in Mark 7:11-13a held the Pharisees responsible for a practice they did not actually promote. Both issues, of the *qorban* vow and the washing of hands, whether or not they accurately portray Pharisaic belief and practice, indicate that the first-century Pharisees impressed their contemporaries with their dedication to the finer points of legal interpretation.

In regard to other, not-legal practices and beliefs, Josephus attempted to provide a Hellenistic frame of reference for his intended readership and wrote that the Pharisees lived their lives according to the dictates of reason (*Ant.* 18.12). In this Josephus directs his Greco-Roman readers' attention to the similarity between the Pharisees, the leading school of thought among the Jews by this time, and the Stoics, the most influential philosophers among the Greeks, a point he deliberately makes elsewhere (*Life* 12).[78] Accordingly, he wrote that Pharisees attribute all things to fate and God while remaining open to human initiative in regard to freedom to choose between right and wrong, fate also participating. This does not seem to have been clear in his mind, since he also took a more deliberately mediate position, suggesting that the Pharisees held that some things are constrained by fate and others by human willing (*War* 2.162-163; *Ant.* 13.172; 18.13).

According to Josephus, Pharisees believed that all souls are immortal. While those who are good go on to "other bodies," the evil suffer unending torment (*War* 2.163; *Ant.* 18.14). The language concerning "the good" is reminiscent of the New Testament concept of resurrection, although it could also suggest reincarnation. We see the former suggestion affirmed by the Acts of the Apostles when the Pharisees join Paul in a dispute against the Sadducees, because of their common belief in the resurrection of the dead (Acts 23:6-9). Josephus suggests that this teaching was especially persuasive with the common folk and was particularly responsible for the Pharisees' popularity with the majority (*Ant.* 18.14-15).

Analysis

It has become an in-house witticism among biblical scholars that we "know" less about Pharisees than we did only thirty or forty years ago, be-

---

[78] Mason, *Flavius Josephus on the Pharisees*, 155.

fore the props of the New Testament, Mishnah, and Josephus were kicked out from their once solid positions and were no longer blindly trusted. That does not imply that we know nothing about them, just much less than we thought we did and would hope to know. The question is, anthropologically speaking, do we have enough information, a "critical mass," so to speak, to be able to work critically with the Scriptures of the New Testament? Do we know enough to critique the generally negative presumptions about the Pharisees therein? Can we, while studying a given passage in Scripture, Josephus, or the Mishnah, determine whether the Pharisees in those passages were behaving or speaking in ways that would be considered "typical" or "representative" of their place in the cultural matrix of early-first-century Palestinian Judaism? The answer I give to this is a cautious yes, in regard to the restricted arena of their amply attested interest in their ancestral traditions, the Law, purity, Sabbath observance, tithing, and public debate. Other broader questions about their beliefs concerning the nature of God, politics, or even ethical concerns remain buried under the silence of the intervening centuries.

The New Testament writers offer, between the lines or in passing, a number of supposed Pharisaic convictions that we can consider briefly, though with a healthy suspicion, since they do not receive wide attestation in Josephus or the Mishnah. The texts suggest that they believed, in accordance with the prophets, that the Messiah would be a descendent of David.[79] They held it to be inappropriate to dine with sinners and those who served as toll collectors for the Romans.[80] Their accusation that Jesus called upon Beelzebul to effect his exorcisms implies that they believed in Beelzebul in the first place, and that humans could call upon this great prince of demons to control lesser demons (Matt 9:32-34; 12:24). It would also seem that some among the Pharisees themselves practiced exorcism (Matt 12:27). They held that only God could forgive sins, and that for a human to claim the capacity to forgive sins was a blasphemy (Luke 5:18-21). They relied upon their ancestry, as descendants of Abraham, to establish a relationship with God (Matt 3:7-10). Another extrapolation from the Gospel of John is that if you baptize you must be either the Messiah, Elijah, or the prophet (John 1:25). When "the prophet" did come, he would *not* arise from Galilee, as did Jesus (John 7:52).

The New Testament writers portray certain Pharisaic behaviors and attitudes that expressed their beliefs in concrete ways. The Pharisees regularly debated publicly about both religious questions and correct behavior

---

[79] Matt 22:41-46; see Isa 11:1-9; Jer 23:5; Ezek 34:23-24.
[80] Mark 2:16//Matt 9:11//Luke 5:30; Luke 15:4.

to verify the validity of teachings.[81] We recall that they discussed the arrival of the Kingdom of God (Luke 17:20), the legality of divorce (Mark 10:2), the necessity of cultic cleansing rituals (Mark 7:1-5//Matt 15:1-2), and, of course, appropriate dining companions.[82] These discussions led to disagreements, not only with Jesus, but also with the Sadducees over the resurrection of the dead.[83] Feelings ran so high at times that people's lives appeared to be in danger (Mark 3:6; Acts 23:6-10). The Pharisees did not live communally, but each in his or her own house (John 7:47, 53), which they maintained, even to the pots, jugs, and bed linens, in ritual purity (Mark 7:3-4). Though they may have been disinclined to dine with sinners and tax collectors, they were known to invite people of public note, including Jesus, to their homes for dinner where they reclined at table, as was fashionable in Greek circles (Luke 7:36-50; 11:37-54; 14:1). In some cases it would seem that the Pharisees were influential in the synagogues (Matt 12:2), and even had some synagogues of their own (Matt 12:9), from which they had the power to expel members, even leaders (John 12:42-43).

The gospels seem unclear on the precise relationship of Pharisees and scribes, at times implying that Pharisees were not scribes but associated with them,[84] and at others that some Pharisees were scribes (Mark 2:16; Luke 5:30; Acts 23:9). It is even possible that there were "scribes of the Pharisees," and perhaps scribes from other Jewish movements as well. Thus one should not assume that every scribe mentioned was from the Pharisaic movement unless specifically stated.

Having begun a process of questioning the New Testament's polemical portrayal, I would continue it here with a fundamental challenge to any presumption that every or even most encounters between Jesus and his Pharisaic contemporaries were necessarily hostile. The textual evidence of the Pharisees and their relationship with the founder of Christianity is quite complicated. Some Pharisees were willing to question the presumption of the majority that Jesus was sinful on the grounds of the signs he performed, inquiring how someone could do what Jesus did and not be from God (John 9:16). They could also be astonished, struck with awe, and moved to glorify God by the clear signs and miracles Jesus worked (Luke 5:17-26). Some among the Pharisees were amazed by Jesus' clever teachings and his capacity to sidestep their skillful attempts to trap him. They went away silenced by Jesus' responses to their crafty questions, and by his

---

[81] Mark 8:11//Matt 12:38; 16:1; John 3:2.
[82] Mark 2:15-16//Matt 9:10-11//Luke 5:30; 15:1-2.
[83] Mark 12:19//Matt 23:32//Luke 20:27; Matt 22:34.
[84] Matt 12:38; 15:1; 23:2-29; Mark 7:1, 5; Luke 5:29-32; 11:53; 15:1-4; John 8:3-9.

own clever questions (Matt 22:41-46). It is not always clear if they departed belligerent in defeat, with grudging respect, or with profound admiration. The Pharisees knew of Herod's intent to kill Jesus, and warned him to flee (Luke 13:31). It is unclear if their counsel was intended as a threat to drive Jesus off or as a well-intentioned warning to save him from destruction. Their ominous intent earlier in the gospel (Luke 6:7, 11) perhaps favors the former reading. Some of the high priests' and Pharisees' own guards found Jesus persuasive (John 7:46). Others among the Pharisees accepted Jesus as a teacher from God (John 3:2). Some even became Christians.[85] During the early formative days in Jerusalem one of their greatest leaders, Gamaliel, convincingly invited his fellow leaders to consider the possibility that the work of the early church was from God (Acts 5:34-39). These points demonstrate that there are cracks in the depiction of all Pharisees as unrelenting critics and opponents of Jesus during his ministry.

Clearly the Pharisees were more than simply observers, but also public proponents of correct behavior, as was also evident in their intervention with Jesus concerning the observance of the Sabbath (Mark 2:23//Matt 12:2//Luke 6:2). At the historical level this controversy and others, more polemic in their final forms, may have originally been no more heated than the theological and practical internal debates of Judaism so common between one rabbi and another, between the houses of Hillel and Shammai, and between Pharisees and Sadducees.[86] As for unity in the midst of disagreement, it should be pointed out, as it is in the Mishnah, that in spite of the differences between the houses of Hillel and Shammai concerning what was impure and what impure, "wherein these declare pure what the others declare impure, neither refrained from using anything that pertained to the others in matters concerned with purity" (*m. Yeb.* 1:4). Supposedly they managed to see past their differences to a shared community life.[87] In fact, some scholars propose that, during the actual life of the historical Jesus, the Pharisees and Jesus' nascent movement may have been perceived as one movement in spite of their differences over purity if they did, in fact, share a common belief in the resurrection.[88] Though this position may be too optimistic, being based on only a few items of convergence, it

---

[85] John 3:1-12; 7:50; 19:39; Acts 15:5; 23:6.

[86] E.g., *m. Bek.* 2:8; *m. Miq.* 4:1; *m. Yad.* 4:7.

[87] There is no intent here to ignore evidence that the house of Shammai was apparently willing, even inclined to violence against the house of Hillel when they were in power.

[88] Joseph Klausner, *Jesus of Nazareth: His Life, Times, and Teaching*, trans. Herbert Danby (New York: Macmillan, 1925) 274.

may still be true that some of the actual historical encounters between Jesus and the Pharisees may, in fact, have been no more hostile than simple intramural dialogue between Jews on matter of import. For example, when the Pharisees question Jesus' practice of dining with sinners it is *possible* to interpret Mark and Matthew's account of their probe as merely polite inquiry (Mark 2:16//Matt 9:11). Luke's gospel, admittedly, is more pointed, suggesting that the Pharisees *murmured* because they *disapproved* of Jesus' behavior (Luke 5:30; 15:4). In this case, since Luke added this touch to his Markan original, we can be confident that it reflects Luke, and not the historical moment.

At the same time, in the Pharisees' defense it should be noted that "eating" and "associating" ought not necessarily be made equivalent. There is a higher degree of cultic interest in how food is chosen, prepared, and consumed than there is in casual meetings in marketplaces and city gates, or joint economic enterprises. Thus one might not eat with someone for cultic reasons and yet do business with them in the marketplace. The claims leveled against Jesus are not that he simply associated with tax collectors and sinners, but that he ate with them (Mark 2:15-16//Matt 9:10-11//Luke 5:30; 15:1-2) and was their *friend* (Matt 11:19//Luke 7:34), implying the intimacy of camaraderie. Before dismissing the Pharisees for their judgmental hard-heartedness we would do well to consider how many people we would choose not to share a meal with or make our friends, and why. Fashions change in this regard. Yesteryears' great industrialists, acclaimed for building up our nation, are this season's pariahs for their rape of the environment and their commodification of human labor. Abortion-providers are heroes to some and murderers to others. Our reasons for the decisions we make seem reasonable to us, according to our standards. It was no different for Pharisees, even acknowledging that Jesus' standards clearly differed from theirs.

Where, then, if a careful reading of the text suggests that Jesus' relationship to the Pharisees was more complex and possibly less hostile than Matthew and John portray it, should we lay the blame for the increased enmity between the two communities, Christian and Pharisaic, that led to the polemics of Matthew and John? As usual history and culture play a huge part. With the destruction of the Temple in Jerusalem and the loss of function by the Sadducees, whose whole purpose, some would suggest, was to function in the Temple and balance Roman dominance with Jewish religious, social, and economic realities, the Pharisees really came into their own. In the subsequent years, just short of the composition of Matthew's, Luke's, and probably John's gospels, the competition between Pharisees and Christians, the two most energetic of the surviving Jewish reform movements, came to a head. Each heatedly contested with the other to re-define the soul of Judaism and how this ancient religion would face a world without a Temple. Though Christianity would ultimately dominate in the Western world as a result of its attraction to and openness toward Gentiles, the Pharisees would succeed in shaping the new Judaism according to their model of worship around a table in the home.

We can see, reading between the lines, that part of their success was at the expense of the participation of Christian Jews in the life of the syna-gogue, sometimes in the fracturing of the relationships between family members and, in a world where imperial recognition of religion was essen-tial, at times in the acceptance of Christianity by the greater world. Once Christians were no longer recognized as Jews they were also no longer protected by the laws of toleration that applied to the Jews. As a result, when Christians refused to worship according to the new imperial religion they were then in various times and places held up as atheists. In this later world (Matt 10:17-18), any intramural discussions between members of the Pharisaic movement and Jesus and his followers would be reinterpreted in light of the pain and suffering of the rejected Christians.

CHAPTER FOUR

Redaction Criticism and the
Development of Luke 7:36-50

The Setting in the Life of Luke

Because the passage we are studying is taken from Luke's gospel, it is desirable to spend a moment on what is unique to Luke's treatment of the Pharisees, for he refers to them with some frequency.[1] As indicated in Chapter One of this book, Luke received much of his material from Mark. We notice that Luke sometimes replicates and occasionally deletes what he finds in Mark concerning the Pharisees, whether the rendering is negative or merely neutral.[2] On occasion Luke softens what he receives, as in Mark 3:5-6 where the Pharisees plot with the Herodians how they might arrange Jesus' death. Luke, while noting that the Pharisees had become enraged, replaces the plotting with a more generalized discussion on what they "might do" to him (Luke 6:5-11). Conversely, Luke also at times intensifies Mark's criticisms, for example, by further clarifying that the "leaven" of the Pharisees was hypocrisy (Mark 8:15//Luke12:1).

Luke also shares distinctive non-Markan material on the Pharisees with Matthew from their source, "Q" (Luke 11:39-45, 53-54//Matt 23:1-22).

---

[1] Luke 5:17, 21, 30, 33; 6:2, 7; 7:30, 36, 37, 39; 11:37, 38, 39, 42, 43, 53; 12:1; 13:31; 14:1, 3; 15:2; 16:14; 17:20; 18:10, 11; 19:39; Acts 5:34; 15:5; 23:6, 7, 8, 9; 26:5.

[2] For the basis for presuming that Luke had access to a copy of the Gospel of Mark that he used as a foundation for writing his own gospel, see Chapter Three of this book. Luke sometimes replicates Mark's negativity (Mark 2:16-17//Luke 5:29-32; 15:1-4) and at other times deletes it (Mark 7:1-13; 8:11; 12:12-17). In Mark 10:2-4, although the command regarding divorce is maintained, the Pharisees do not prompt the issue with a question. Where Mark is neutral, Luke normally replicates the neutrality (Mark 2:18//Luke 5:33; Mark 2:23-24//Luke 6:1-5. In this latter instance Luke shifts from Mark's "the Pharisees" to the less comprehensive "some of the Pharisees").

This latter material contains some of the most resoundingly negative information on the Pharisees in the New Testament. At the same time, while we can only make educated guesses whether Luke shortened his material or Matthew lengthened his, Matthew indisputably goes on at much greater length in berating the Pharisees for their failings than does Luke. This does not soften the negativity of the data Luke included, but it suggests that Luke's context was further removed from Judaism in general, and Pharisaism in particular, than was Matthew's.

There are also distinctly Lukan portrayals of the Pharisees, some of which are from his own unique source "L."[3] Luke also creatively inserts them into episodes he shares with Mark, or with Matthew in "Q," from which they were originally absent, at times identifying heretofore unnamed bystanders as Pharisees.[4] Luke also so significantly alters received material from these sources that may or may not have originally included the Pharisees that he virtually creates new episodes.[5] It is in this last group that our pericope, Luke 7:36-50, belongs.

It is difficult to discern a pattern in these later unique or altered texts. Luke's unique information is sometimes negative, such as when Luke clarifies that the Pharisees love money; neutral, for example, when they ask information seeking questions; and even potentially positive, as in the case where they give Jesus a thoughtful warning of Herod's intent to murder him. In the case of Luke 7:36-50, Luke has chosen to identify Simon as a Pharisee, a detail lacking in all the other accounts. Curiously, though, he fails to include in the story any of the most common beliefs or religious observances one expects from a Pharisee. Also missing is any observable element of the typical anti-Pharisaic polemic that runs so consistently through so many passages.

Recognizing the complexity of the textual development of each of the gospels, it is particularly important that, when reading the gospels, modern readers not superimpose the more hostile tenor of Matthew's and John's accounts of the Pharisees onto Luke's, or conflate Mark's and John's profoundly different accounts of a woman's anointing of Jesus in Bethany with Luke's in Nain. In fact, as a general interpretive principle, after we have mined each of the gospels for the cultural material it is best that we allow each gospel to stand on its own. The end product of maintaining this careful distinction is that we will end up with four distinct perspectives on the person of Jesus and his teaching. As any forensic investigator will attest,

---

[3] Luke 7:29-30; 13:31-32; Acts 5:30-40; 15:4-6; 23:3-10.
[4] Luke 13:31-32; 17:20; 19:38-40.
[5] Luke 5:17-26; 7:36-50.

four distinct witnesses who have not been tampered with are better than one bland, composite perspective. Toward this end, we will now begin the process of setting out what is unique in Luke's gospel for its own sake, and contrasting his version of the dinner at Simon's house with those from the other gospels in the pursuit of Luke's uniqueness.

We begin with the person of Luke. While we do, note that our redactional analysis and our deliberately anthropological focus will overlap and aid each other in the pursuit of understanding the text. The gospel, unfortunately, provides no biographical detail concerning its author. Authors usually leave self-revelatory details in the texts they produce, unless of course they set out to deceive. We will have to make all our determinations about the person of Luke from the evidence in his gospel and the Acts of the Apostles, which he is also believed to have written. For example, as a writer, his proficiency with written Greek vocabulary, grammar, and style, as well as his ample knowledge of the Greek version of the Hebrew Bible, revealed by his frequent references and quotations, all suggest that, as regards literacy, he was not simply a town scribe but a man of the upper economic strata, with the resources to obtain a superior education and time for the leisurely study of religious texts. Thus through his use of language alone we can determine that he was well educated, probably urbane, and economically advantaged, and stylistically rooted in the Greco-Roman world of the late first century C.E.

When we move to the question of content and sympathies, we see Luke striving to make room for Gentiles in the heavenly dispensation of Jesus,[6] even making the mission to the Gentiles a part of the commissioning that closes the gospel (Luke 24:47), something that is then carried out from chapter 13 of Acts to its end. Opinions of scholars vary, some holding that Luke was a Hellenized Jew living in the Diaspora, others that he was originally a Gentile who converted to Judaism or at least was very attracted to the Jewish religion before he became a Christian. The starting position for this work is that Luke was probably a Gentile convert to Christianity who had a profound appreciation for Judaism and the Greek version of the Jewish Bible, that is, the Septuagint.[7]

---

[6] E.g., Luke 2:29-35; 4:25-27; Acts 10; 15. Compare Matthew's genealogy (1:1-17) with Luke's (3:23-38), and consider how Luke's ending Jesus' line with Adam implies a different sense of inclusiveness than does Matthew's beginning of his with Abraham. Ponder whether Luke's deletion of Mark's story of the Syro-Phoenician woman (Mark 7:25-30), where Jesus refers to Gentiles as "dogs," was a part of the larger project of accommodating the Christian message to the Gentile world.

[7] For a detailed analysis of the question of Luke's ethnicity see Joseph A. Fitzmyer, *The Gospel According to Luke I–IX* (New York: Doubleday, 1979) 41–47.

This much being said, the person of Luke remains mysterious and at a distance. We do not know his family, city of origin, or early religious experience. We do not know if he married and had children. We do not even know his real name, "Luke" having been assigned to this text in the early second century.[8] Even so, Luke's identity as a Greek Gentile is an important datum even for studying the meaning of the dinner at Simon the Pharisee's house, in the town of Nain where the meal presumably took place, in the region of the Galilee. We cannot simply presume that Luke's narrative is a window into the first-century world in which all the social roles (e.g., host, guest, woman in public) reflect Galilean or Judean perspectives. In fact, there are good reasons for questioning Luke's accuracy in replicating first-century Palestinian culture and history. In part this is because of Luke's willingness to adapt his sources. As we saw in the first chapter, Luke significantly and consistently shaped his narrative to place events in what he considered a reasonable order, one that is "sensible" rather than "historical," and to reflect his theology.

We can also detect from his gospel that Luke is not particularly well informed when it comes to Judean or Galilean geography. For example, a glance at any map of Palestine, attending to the distances involved, will demonstrate the improbability of Luke's placement of Jesus almost simultaneously in the synagogues of Judea and at the Sea of Gennesaret, also called the Sea of Galilee (Luke 4:44–5:1). This error and others like it lead most scholars to conclude that Luke had never visited Palestine and lived at some distance from it, with some suggesting hypothetically that he lived somewhere in Syria. We further note that Luke consistently ignores items of local Palestinian cultural interest that surface in the other gospels and, apart from "amen," avoids the use of Hebrew or Aramaic terminology. This really is not surprising. When we take into account our cultural principles from Chapter Two above, both the permeability and the distinctiveness of cultural boundaries, we may well wonder if Luke's knowledge of Judean and Palestinian culture was any more accurate than his geography. Compounding this doubt, we also note that Luke's social location among the elite, advantaged class and his further geographical remove suggest that, in

---

[8] Since "Luke" is an ancient attribution for the composer of the Third Gospel, even though the actual identity of this author is uncertain, this book uses the name to refer to whatever person was responsible for the final composition of the Gospel of Luke. While reading and writing norms from the first century do not *demand* that "Luke" was male, they would suggest that it was much more likely. This work will operate within the bounds of the overwhelming probabilities, though serious scholars have posited that certain New Testament writings, including Luke's gospel, could have been authored by women.

writing about the lives of Palestinian peasants and their religious leaders, Jesus and Simon, Luke was writing about a social class not properly his own.

How well, you may ask yourself, does an American *understand* the neighboring culture of Mexico, or the English-speaking Canadian that of the French-speaking? Also ask how accurately an "alien" can literarily represent any other culture without having been steeped in it. Even though Luke used Palestinian *place names* and *characters* such as "Nain," "Galilee," "Jesus," and "Simon the Pharisee," we may ask: was Luke in fact representing *events* as they would have been carried out in Galilee, or is it not even more likely that they reflect the culture of Luke's place of origin? Where else, culturally, could Luke set the events if not in the culture he was most familiar with, that is, his own? The more Luke altered a given text, in fact, the more he risked stripping it of its originating culture's influence. Luke 7:36-50 is one of the passages Luke received from Mark that he most profoundly reworked. Thus in regard to the social location of Simon the Pharisee's dinner party in Luke 7:36-50, we might do better to ask what it meant for a person of public stature to invite notable guests to dinner in the larger Hellenized world from which we presume Luke sprang.

On the other hand, since the cultural worlds of Judean peasantry and the larger Hellenistic world had collided, we admittedly need to approach this question from the opposite direction, that is, the permeability of cultures. The conquests of Alexander the Great in the third century B.C.E. had imposed Hellenistic influence on the Near East. By the time Jesus was an adult, even areas long settled by Jews were influenced by centuries of contact with Hellenistic language, religion, architecture, theater, philosophical values, and literature. The hapless efforts of the Jews to resist the occasionally oppressive imposition of this culture are recorded in 1 and 2 Maccabees. Ironically, within only a couple of generations the descendants of this great struggle had adopted "Alexander" as a common first name. Even the most ardent defenders of Jewish culture were unconsciously influenced by Hellenism's cultural impact. Therefore we will need to remain conscious that, though Luke's world was probably not conscious of Palestinian concerns, Jesus' Palestinian world had been greatly influenced by Luke's Greco-Roman milieu.

In a healthy tension between fidelity and creativity, the final text of a work such as any of the gospels will inevitably reflect the writer's cultural perspective to some degree, greater or lesser, depending on the level of the writer's intrusiveness. Thus we can expect Luke's original source material for this passage to interface with Luke's culture, with its presumptions of appropriate roles and settings for its participants, helping to shape the final version of this text.

Luke 7:36-50 and Mark 14:3-9//Matt 26:6-13//John 12:1-9

Our consideration of the background to Luke and his gospel was, admittedly, brief and sketchy for the sake of moving to the proper focus of this book, which is Luke 7:36-50. Similar narratives are told not only in Mark 14:3-9 and its parallel version in Matt 26:6-13, as often happens, but also in John 12:1-8. Since the Gospel of John relies on an independent stream of tradition apart from the synoptic gospels, and only occasionally overlaps their content, those few times when it happens give us a particularly rich opportunity to study the tradition's process of adaptation.

In all four versions Jesus, while eating in a home, is anointed by a silent woman. In each case her actions are a cause of controversy among the other guests, and in every instance Jesus comes to her defense. Part of what makes this study so interesting, though, is that Luke 7:36-50 is also very unlike these other seemingly parallel narratives. In the synoptic gospels the meal and anointing take place in the home of Simon. Luke identifies Simon as a Pharisee, while Mark and Matthew refer to him as a leper. In contrast, in John's gospel there is no mention of Simon as either a leper or a Pharisee since the meal takes place in the home of Martha, Mary, and Lazarus. Although the synoptic gospels fail to identify the woman, Luke's narrator informs us that she is "a sinner in the city." John, uniquely, identifies her as Mary, the sister of Lazarus and Martha. Curiously, in John 12:1-8 Martha serves the dinner guests while Mary attends to Jesus, anointing his feet, a situation vaguely paralleling another story in Luke 10:38-42 where Martha complains to Jesus that she has been abandoned in her responsibilities to serve while Mary remained seated, again at Jesus' feet. One has to wonder if the similarities between these two narratives suggest a connection between them at an earlier stage of their development.

While Luke is not precise about the geographical location of the meal, one might draw the conclusion that Simon's house was in Nain, a town in Galilee and Jesus' last identifiable position, from which he does not seem to have departed (Luke 7:11). Mark, Matthew, and John all identify the site much farther south in Bethany, a town in Judea only a short distance from Jerusalem, a setting completely irreconcilable with Luke's geography. All four gospels agree that Jesus was dining when he was anointed, though Mark, Matthew, and Luke further specify that he was reclined at the table, a common posture for men at formal public meals in the Greco-Roman world, and not unheard of in the very Hellenized Judean culture as well. John is silent on the matter.

In both Mark and Matthew the woman pours the ointment on his *head,* while in Luke and John she anoints and dries his *feet* with her hair. In

John, Mary, dry-eyed, anoints Jesus' feet and then wipes off the excess ointment with her hair. According to Luke the woman was weeping, and after tears "rained" on his feet she wiped them with her hair, and only then anointed them with the ointment.

In Mark, Matthew, and John the controversy swirls around the issue of waste. The ointment, specifically nard in Mark and John, is expensive (Matthew), costly, and pure (Mark). Both Mark and John specify its worth as three hundred denarii.[9] Mark, Matthew, and Luke all indicate that the ointment came in an alabaster flask, suggesting that the container was also expensive. Different individuals, guests in Mark, the disciples in Matthew, and Judas Iscariot in John, react indignantly to the cost of the ointment. They all suggest that it should have been sold and the proceeds given to the poor. Judas, it is implied in John, would have benefited by taking a cut from the sale.

It is in this regard that Luke's version goes farthest afield. Though the ointment is brought in an alabaster container, Luke's version fails to refer to the ointment's cost, its possible sale, or any benefit for the poor. Alone among the evangelists, Luke designates the woman a sinner, allowing her ministrations to take on a suggestive coloration not noted by the other evangelists. It apparently seemed to Simon, in the context of the apparently public meal he was hosting, that the woman's presence and behavior suggested she was a prostitute. Jesus' willingness to permit such a person to touch him in that fashion was an indication to Simon that Jesus could not have been the prophet Simon had seemingly hoped he might be (Luke 7:16). The implication of Simon's musings was that a prophet would not allow such a person to publicly touch him in such an intimate fashion.

In John's version the meal is specifically six days before Passover, immediately preceding Jesus' triumphal entry into Jerusalem. Similarly, in both Mark and Matthew the meal was held just shortly before Passover, and immediately before Judas Iscariot made his arrangements to betray Jesus to the chief priests. Although, in John, Judas does not leave the meal to plot with the chief priests, the priests do plot Lazarus' death because many people were coming to believe in Jesus because of Lazarus' resuscitation (John 11:1-46). Thus the incident was intimately connected to the events that led up to Jesus' death in Mark, Matthew, and John. This connection is made explicit when Jesus affirms the woman's actions as a preparation for his impending death and burial. This element is completely

---

[9] A single denarius was worth a day's wage for a common laborer. Thus after Sabbaths and holy days had been factored in the ointment was worth a year's salary.

lacking in Luke's gospel, since he places the event only a third of the way into his story, while Jesus is still engaged in his Galilean ministry, fully two chapters before he even sets out toward Jerusalem (Luke 9:51).

Redaction criticism, while not neglecting what is typical or shared, focuses on those areas that are unique and show the highest probability of being editorial activity in order to highlight what is *uniquely* or *distinctively* Lukan, reflective of his community, or evidential of its particular needs. For this reason it will be necessary to investigate the development of Luke 7:36-50, distinguishing those elements of Luke's material that are dependent on the various traditions he received from Mark or shared in some way with John from those that are unique to Luke or evidence the clearest probability of originating from Luke's creativity. The last two will hopefully provide us with insight into Luke's special perspective.

Since Matthew's version is a separate though faithful strain of development of Mark's account, making only minor editorial changes to tighten up Mark's wordiness and fine tune his grammar, demonstrating no independent influence beyond Matthew's editorial preferences, there is no particular need to include Matthew in further comparison. Luke, though, was far less loyal to Mark's account. Contrary to expectations, Luke's version has only the ten following areas of commonality with Mark: (1) the anointing of Jesus (2) by an uninvited, (3) unnamed (4) woman, (5) the meal setting, at which Jesus is reclined, (6) the use of myrrh (7) in an alabaster flask, (8) the host's name, "Simon," (9) a reaction from the spectators, and (10) Jesus' defense of the woman.[10] With regard to John, Luke shares eight areas of commonality, (1) (4) (5) (6) (9) and (10) above, and two exclusive details: (11) the anointing of the feet and (12) the drying of the feet with the woman's hair.

A careful analysis of the similarities and dissimilarities among the three pertinent accounts, Mark, Luke, and John, reveals that, with no fewer than thirty-four possible points of similarity, Luke only agrees with both of the others six times, in that (1) Jesus was anointed (4) by a woman (5) at a meal (6) with myrrh, (9) followed by some element of faulty assessment of the woman's actions by the witnesses, and (10) a defense of the woman by Jesus.

Altogether, these areas of mutual agreement are fewer than the eleven similarities shared by Mark and John, but not by Luke. These include (13) a location in Bethany, (14) the great expense (15) of the more specific nard, (16) an evaluation by a witness that the anointing was a waste, (17) the clarification that the nard was worth three hundred denarii, (18) the accu-

---

[10] Fitzmyer, *Luke,* 684.

sation that the nard ought to have been sold, and (19) the suggestion that the proceeds ought to have gone to the poor. (20) Jesus instructs the woman's critic(s) to leave her alone (21) since the anointing was a preparation for his burial. Jesus continues (22) with almost identical terminology that "you have the poor with you always" and (23) in exactly the same way "but you do not always have me." It is precisely in these eleven non-Lukan areas of agreement that the primary points of Mark's and John's versions are made, that the woman's anointing of Jesus was not a waste, but a preparation for his death.

Additionally, Luke has eleven unique points, critical to the development of the essential message of his narrative: (24) the presence of a Pharisee, (25) the identity of the woman as a sinner, (26) her weeping, (27) the "raining" of her tears on Jesus' feet, (28) her drying of the tears, (29) and kissing of the feet, (30) the parable of the debtors, (31) Jesus' words on love, (32) his forgiveness of the woman's sins, (33) the wonderment of the guests at the identity of one who can forgive sins, and (34) Jesus' farewell declaration, "go in peace." In this regard it is noteworthy that the unique points of Luke's version reflect themes of sinfulness, faith, forgiveness, and love, hallmarks of Luke's unique material and editorial activity in the rest of his gospel.

From this analysis, highlighting the significant differences between Luke's account and the other three, and after finding only small variations among these other three, one could easily conclude that, while Luke's story is based on traditions shared in part with the other evangelists, it became, through a process of conflation and editing, a largely *different* story than the one the others tell.[11]

Theories for Luke's Unique Narrative

Operating from the majority scholarly position that the multiple-source theory is largely correct, we must presume that Luke had access to Mark 14:3-9. It is equally clear, however, from the differences between Luke 7:36-60 and Mark 14:3-9, that Luke did not view Mark's portrayal as fundamentally definitive. Any worthy theory of redaction will have to address Luke's dissatisfaction with both the point of the Markan version and its narrative placement, before the preparations for the Passover at the end of Mark's gospel, since Luke essentially modified the first and completely

---

[11] This analysis is based, in large part, on the work of Luke Timothy Johnson, but with significant modifications; see his *Luke* SP 3 (Collegeville: The Liturgical Press, 1991) 128–29.

abandoned the second. It will also have to explain the additional material unique to Luke's version.

There are at least three hypotheses for the differences between Luke's version and Mark's. The first is that Luke himself was responsible for both the alterations and the additional, unique material, having composed them himself. The second is that he borrowed the unique material from a supplementary non-Markan source, either written or oral, and edited his Markan version to fit this additional material. The third option, a combination of the first two, is that Luke borrowed some of his unique material and composed the rest, with varying degrees of either being possible.

There is more than a hint, in the similarities between Luke's version and John's, that the first option is not probable. That both Luke and John should coincidentally invent a story in which a woman anointed Jesus' feet and wiped them with her hair does not seem likely. It is more likely that they shared some common tradition about a foot anointing. This possibility is made all the more likely since there are other places of overlap between these two gospels, though not enough to indicate that either had a copy of the other at hand.[12] A source, shared between them, simply makes better sense of their commonalities. This hypothetical common source, as far as Luke is concerned, would have constituted one small part of what we referred to above as "L," that is, those traditions available to Luke independently from Mark, responsible for Luke's non-Markan, non-"Q" material.

In regard to the relationship between "L" and John, there is much we do not know. There are no extant editions of this latter source, leaving us uncertain as to its extent, if it came to Luke in oral or written form, in one document or many, or how far it was coextensive with the similar source drawn upon by John.[13] Among those things we would like to know, but do not, regarding the material where Luke and John were both distinct from each other, is which of the two more faithfully represented the content of that shared resource, or if all the differences resulted from Luke's and John's creativity. Either Luke or John or both could have altered portions of this tradition to make it fit into their narrative, either by shortening, adding, or further conflating it with yet other traditions. Even careful analysis can only suggest whether the material in Luke's gospel that is found in neither Mark's nor John's version came to Luke as part of "L" or resulted from Lukan creativity. Clearly, there is much we do not know.

---

[12] For more on similarities between Luke and John see Raymond E. Brown, *The Gospel According to John: I–XII* (Garden City, NY: Doubleday, 1966) xliv–xlvii.

[13] François Bovon argues that Luke 7:36-50 probably came to Luke from oral tradition as part of his special, unique source: *L'Evangile selon Saint Luc, 1–9*. CNT 3a (Geneva: Labor et Fides, 1991) 378–79.

We can, however, say with some confidence, in light of what *is* shared by Luke with Mark and by Luke with John, that Luke's version represents what is technically called a conflation, or combining, of traditions, merging at least two anointing episodes, Mark 14:3-9 and "L," and including however much editing was required to make a smooth narrative fit between the two and, perhaps, some of Luke's own creative compositional work.

There is more than one way to explain how two distinct anointing traditions came to circulate in the early Christian traditions about Jesus. The simplest, though not incontestable, hypothesis is that these two versions sprang from some original anointing tradition, diversely adapted and combined with additional traditions, either by their initial oral transmitters or by the different evangelists, leading to the diverse expressions found in the gospels.[14] Another possibility is that Luke's version, which is the most distinctive of the three present in the gospels, representing a completely different anointing tradition, came to him largely intact.[15] One popular explanation along this line proposes that there were originally two separate events. In the first, a sinful woman enters the house of a Galilean Pharisee while Jesus is reclined at table. There she weeps, and when the tears fall on Jesus' feet, she wipes them with her hair, provoking comment. In the second, a woman anoints Jesus' head while he is at the house of Simon the leper, in Bethany. These two traditions were joined at the level of oral tradition, coming intact to Luke as a story in which Jesus' feet are anointed.[16]

Some readers will inevitably be concerned that these sources, Mark 14:3-9 and "L," and, for that matter, the one used by John, be rooted in some historical reality. It is not, however, critical for purposes of redaction criticism whether they originated from the same historical events or that they be rooted in a historical event at all, since the primary focus is on the implications of Luke's editorial activity. Thus we will spend no time attempting to reconstruct what that event or events looked like, or determining which, or even if any, of the gospel accounts of a woman anointing Jesus is more likely to accurately report that theoretically historical event. That is a worthy, but different, project. Too many layers of development lie between the actual life of Jesus and the final recording of this particular event in any of the gospels for us to undertake historical research lightly. Nor, in a redaction study of Luke's account, is it essential to study separately each of the various older traditions he used, in an atomistic sense, as

---

[14] Kathleen E. Corley, *Private Women, Public Meals: Social Conflict in the Synoptic Tradition* (Peabody, MA: Hendrickson, 1993) 103; C. H. Dodd, *Historical Tradition in the Fourth Gospel* (Cambridge: Cambridge University Press, 1963) 162–73.

[15] Johnson, *Luke*, 128–29.

[16] See Fitzmyer, *Luke*, 685–86.

items in themselves, since the intent is to understand Luke's overall vision and place of origin.[17] If, for a moment, we trace the development of a given tradition and, in particular, Luke's hand in that development, it is primarily to gain insight into Luke's particular interests, theology, overarching themes, and community of origin by the alterations he makes in his received traditions.

The most interesting aspect of the similarities between Luke's and John's versions is that they represent the most awkward details of their accounts. As already stated, it is almost certain that those features shared by Luke and John, that is, the anointing of feet as opposed to the head and the wiping of Jesus' feet with the woman's hair, in light of their challenging, discomforting quality, would not have been arrived at separately and coincidentally by both authors.[18] Thus these two items would most likely not originate with, but predate Luke. In fact, this similarity even suggests that Luke's version, in certain particulars, may actually be more faithful to any original tradition than Mark's. It is easier, in this case, to explain how at some point either Mark or his source, uncomfortable with the sexual connotations of a woman anointing Jesus' feet, altered the story, substituting the much safer "head" for "feet," than it would be to explain the reverse, that Luke and John independently introduced this peculiar twist. This is especially so since there is no emphasis given to Mary's choice of "feet" over "head" in John's version.[19]

These two items, the anointing and wiping of feet, are the fundamental turning points of Luke's version. Everything that happens prior to them is primarily scene setting. Everything that happens subsequently is either an interpretation or consequence of them. Thus by virtue of narrative weight this non-Markan material really serves as the essential tradition for Luke's version.

Narrative Placement in Luke's Gospel

Even though we can see that Luke's anointing story has made a radically different point than the Markan version, they were apparently similar enough to each other that Luke chose not to include both. Furthermore, he chose not to insert his version in the same narrative location, or context, immediately before the preparations for the celebration of the Passover in

---

[17] Evelyn R. Thibeaux, "'Known to Be a Sinner': The Narrative Rhetoric of Luke 7:36-50," *BTB* 23 (1993) 152.

[18] John 12:3//Luke 7:38.

[19] Fitzmyer's preferred option: *Luke,* 686.

Jerusalem and preceding the Passion narrative, as did Mark. Since context plays such an important role in understanding the meaning of a passage, if we desire to understand the full implication of how Luke 7:36-50 differs from Mark 14:3-9 we need to consider both how the old setting failed to suit Luke's narrative purposes and how Luke's new narrative placement succeeded in serving his greater ends.

In regard to the latter question, as already pointed out, Luke, in following the project of offering an account that was "accurate and in sequence" (Luke 1:3), on occasion deliberately rearranged Mark's account to serve his own narrative sense of what was sequentially sensible. When Luke placed the anointing in the first third of his gospel, as opposed to the last fifth as in the Markan sequence, we have to presume it was not simply coincidental, but every bit as deliberate as every other change he made.

Luke had a significant amount of independent material, roughly sixty percent of his gospel, that he inserted into his Markan outline. In addition to the infancy narratives in chapters 1 and 2, and smaller insertions throughout, Luke made two sizable insertions into the material he received from Mark, at Luke 6:20–8:3 and 9:5–18:14, referred to commonly as the "little" and "big interpolations." The narrative placement of Luke 7:36-50 in the little interpolation, in association with other non-Markan material, further supports the suggestion that Luke's version comes from an independent tradition although it does not necessitate it.

The anointing at Simon the Leper's house served as the first episode in Mark's Passion narrative. Jesus himself associates the woman's anointing with the preparations for his death and burial. This suited Mark's unrelentingly bleak depiction of Jesus' last days, acknowledging the inevitability of decay, the mystery of an empty tomb, and the silent fear of the women, who flee, saying nothing to anyone. Luke's death and burial, on the other hand, are hardly so desolate. God would triumph in the resurrection. In this light Jesus was confident, and anointings were superfluous. Thus the setting in and purpose for which Mark uses the woman's anointing were not suited to Luke's reworked Passion and death. If Luke were to use this passage, and the opportunity it offered to instruct the reader in the proper understanding of the woman's actions, he had to find an alternative setting and contrast, something he apparently felt quite free to do. Luke's much earlier placement of this pericope in his gospel gives Luke the opportunity to change Mark's portrayal of Jesus' opponents, focusing especially in the passages preceding this episode (6:11; 7:30-34) on the Pharisees.[20] Luke

[20] John J. Kilgallen, "A Proposal for Interpreting Luke 7:36-50," *Biblica* 72 (1991) 315–16.

tempers and reshapes the apparent opposition of the Pharisees, as indicated by the very evenhanded treatment Simon receives from Jesus. This may well imply a complicated relationship between Luke's community and the Pharisees in which, in spite of apparent official group opposition to Christianity, some Pharisees were even known to have become Christians (Acts 15:5). Furthermore, Luke chose to place this account of the woman's repentance and forgiveness in such a way that it served as a counterpart to the subsequent passage in which women who had been cured and exorcized responded by supporting the ministry of Jesus (8:1-3). Both pericopes served as examples for the following parable of the sower, mutually demonstrating in the lives of these women both what it was to be fertile ground for the reception of the word of God and how one could bear abundant fruit with a good heart and patient endurance.[21]

Luke's Redacting, Editorial Activity

The most easily recognized evidence of editorial activity is precisely what we've been discussing, the inclusion of or, more technically, conflation of details from Mark's account of a woman who anoints Jesus on the head with a non-Markan, presumably pre-existing narrative of a woman anointing Jesus on the feet, from the putative resource "L." We recognize this endeavor based on the resemblance of Luke's version to what, with certain knowledge, we know is found in Mark's version, and the reasonable assumption that Luke had a source that resembled some small amount of material also available to John.

With regard to Luke's unique material, however, there is also internal evidence suggesting that either Luke or an earlier redactor combined at least two distinct traditions, forming them into a new story, and then provided the necessary linking material to tie it together. In the first place, the parable gives an account of two defaulting financial debtors, and their creditor's willingness to set aside what was due. This seems to some scholars only awkwardly suited as a metaphor either explaining or contrasting the activities of the sinful woman with Simon's hospitality. If the parable stood alone, independent of this passage, it would have made a different point, e.g., that sinners, whether great or small, find themselves unable to redeem themselves. Nevertheless, God's magnanimous forgiveness is available to sinners, great and small alike. Only the interpretation, 7:47a-c, provided at a marked distance from the parable at 7:41-42, directs the parable's meaning toward the varying degrees of gratitude one might expect. This suggests

---

[21] Ibid. 317.

at least the possibility that this parable had a prior existence independent of its current narrative location and explanation.

Although it is possible that Luke may have composed the parable, few scholars suggest it. In this case it is more likely that the parable was a received tradition and that only the explanatory verses were "creatively" composed to bridge the anointing with the parable. When we reread Luke's original mission statement for his composition (Luke 1:1-4), we see that he desired to write a more orderly and accurate account of the traditions that had been handed down by those he believed were eyewitnesses. While that is a different project than the composition of new material, it does not prohibit drawing sensible conclusions from received traditions that he thought were poorly clarified in their original expressions. In any case, whoever combined the parable with the anointing tradition, be it Luke or someone before him, would most likely have been responsible for the explanatory verses.

A second area of concern is the lack of clarity about whether the woman's love was the cause or the result of her forgiveness. At 7:47a-c we recognize that the woman was the debtor with the greater liability. The Greek terminology would normally be read to imply that the woman's actions led to her forgiveness: "*because* she loved much." This makes sense of the forgiveness expressed by Jesus in v. 48. This, however, was not the point of the parable, which was that her acts of love were her expressions of gratitude since she had already received pardon for her sins. It is possible, though not intuitive, to translate the Greek as "hence" or "as a result she loved much." This, too, is awkward, since no recorded words of forgiveness are directed to her until late in this passage, at 7:48, well after the woman initiated her actions. Why would Jesus say there that her sins were forgiven if he has already made the point that her actions were an expression of gratitude for forgiveness received? What did Luke intend? Serious scholars line up on both sides of the implication of the woman's ministry to Jesus.[22]

If anything is certain, it is that Luke, though fallible, was a careful editor. It seems likely that, as skilled as he was in communicating, he would have recognized and corrected any inherent contradictions in his received traditions, as he so carefully demonstrated with his Markan material. It also seems quite unlikely that he would have combined his traditions into a narrative that did not make sense. With this in mind, we can see

---

[22] Fitzmyer, *Luke,* 691–92; Ben Witherington III, *Women in the Ministry of Jesus: A Study of Jesus' Attitudes to Women and their Roles as Reflected in His Earthly Life* (New York: Cambridge University Press, 1984) 55–56.

that it makes better sense, at the interpretive level, to seek an understanding of the passage that is cogent rather than inept or contradictory.[23]

Toward that end, it may be possible to interpret Jesus' parable too narrowly. The suggestions that the woman's love could only be either the cause or result of forgiveness may be simply too neat and orderly for the range of human possibilities.[24] The woman's great love could have been a response not simply to an act of forgiveness, but to the whole of Jesus' ministry, recognizing in it the key to the liberation she desired. As a debtor, like the one who owed the three hundred days' wages, she stood before her creditor having come to appreciate, through Jesus' actions and preaching, the nature of her own relationship with him. Such was her confidence, knowing already that the freedom she longed for would be hers, that she could respond with *precipitous* gratitude. Thus Jesus' expressed words of forgiveness in v. 48 were merely a confirmation of what the woman had already begun to experience as a result of Jesus' ministry. So it is today for Christians who approach God in prayer or, more particularly, Catholics who repentantly seek the ministry of a priest in the confessional, desiring God's forgiveness. The act is conceived of, initiated, and brought to completion, overshadowed by a grateful confidence that forgiveness will be granted. The counterbalance to this point in the parable was that one who stood in lesser bondage to sin or oppression, even having heard and appropriated the same message of release, would respond differently, with less enthusiasm.

However this problem is solved, the very controversies over the imprecise relationship of the woman's actions and her forgiveness and the, at best, awkward lack of clear correlation between the parable and the rest of the account seem to suggest, again, that certain elements of this story, the parable in particular, existed independently from the rest of Luke's anointing narrative and only came to their current significance with their present narrative locations.

While it is not impossible that "L" placed the event in the house of "Simon," that seems unnecessarily speculative, since we know that Luke's Markan source had set this narrative in the house of "Simon the leper," whereas there is no "Simon" in the only other anointing tradition in John.[25] We note, however, that the narrator in both Mark and Matthew named Simon in the opening verse of the passage while establishing the setting.

---

[23] Ibid. 54.

[24] Eric Franklin, *Luke: Interpreter of Paul, Critic of Matthew* (Sheffield: JSOT Press, 1994) 203.

[25] Fitzmyer suggests that the name Simon could have been appended to Luke's narrative before Luke received it (*Luke,* 688).

Curiously, Simon's name is not revealed in Luke's version until 7:40, by which point the meal has progressed, the woman has initiated her activity, and "the Pharisee," as yet unnamed, has drawn the conclusion that Jesus is not a prophet. Jesus, not the narrator, is the first to mention Simon's name, and he does so in an address to "Simon" that is *not* Markan in origin. Fitzmyer suggests that Luke's conflation of the stories is responsible for the delay in actually naming Simon.[26]

We cannot be sure whether Luke introduced the information that Simon was a Pharisee, as opposed to a leper as in Mark, or drew this information from his source, "L." The best evidence, perhaps, that Luke himself was responsible would be the way Luke handles Pharisees and dining elsewhere in his gospel. Either way we have to ask ourselves: does the fact that Simon was a Pharisee affect how we should interpret the meal or not? Each of the gospels has its own way of dealing with the question of Pharisees, but they consistently portray them as Jesus' opponents, confronting him for his failure to observe the Sabbath, violating the Law and rituals of purity, and associating with the disreputable.[27] None but the last of these issues arises during the meal at Simon's house. The bathing rituals we presume are customary for Pharisees are pointedly *not* mentioned here. Concern for ritual purity, for which there are ample prompts in the narrative (e.g., washing, possible implications of sexual defilement, an allegedly unclean "guest" at a meal, etc.) are also markedly absent, but this fits in with Luke's larger editorial pattern. Luke deals with these Jewish customs briefly at Luke 11:37-54, which seems to be his sole summary and dismissive statement on the subject of ritual purity and defilement.[28] Since Luke tends not to repeat himself too often, it is not a surprise that they do not arise here as well. Even the way Luke handles the question of Jesus dining and socializing with tax collectors and sinners (Luke 5:29-32; 7:34) seems to reflect more concern for the social implications of such associations than any

---

[26] Ibid. 685.

[27] Eating with tax collectors and sinners: Mark 2:16-17; Matt 9:11-15; Luke 5:29-32; 15:1-4. Observance of the Sabbath: Mark 2:23-24; Matt 12:1-3, 9-14; Luke 6:1-11; 14:1-8. The Law: Mark 10:2-4; Matt 19:3-8. Ritual purity: Mark 7:1-13; Matt 15:1-10; 23:24-28; Luke 11:37-40.

[28] True, Jesus does cleanse a leper of his uncleanness at Luke 5:12-15, and refers to this activity in 7:22. These references are almost certainly more properly understood as instances of Jesus' role as one who proclaims good news and liberator of the poor, demonstrating Jesus' fulfillment of Luke 7:17-19, than it is of any particular Lukan interest in issues of ritual purity as such. In fact, one of the major complaints Jesus will voice in ch. 11 is the way that Pharisees and scribes have misplaced their religious focus, placing their attention more on such items rather than alms, judgment, and love of God. He does not oppose the interest altogether, allowing that they should not neglect those other things (v. 42d).

awareness of potential defilement. That being the case, it seems unnecessary to insert issues of purity into this meal setting, since Luke does not make them the point.

Since purity is not an issue, and since Simon does not act in a hostile fashion to coincide with the polemical tone of Luke's received traditions, we may well wonder why Luke chose to alter Simon's identity from leper to Pharisee. Since it seems most likely that Luke was, in fact, responsible for the alteration, this one small change may express more clearly Luke's actual opinion of individual Pharisees than the preformed traditions he received. Simon's behavior, welcoming Jesus into his home, dialoguing with him politely, failing to understand the meanings of events, but responding graciously and attentively to continued teaching and reflection, echoes the overall picture of Pharisees so far as they are mentioned in Acts 15, where Luke consciously includes them in v. 22.

Because the issue of "the poor" is so significant in the Markan and Johannine narratives and is so visibly lacking from Luke 7:36-50, we need to consider the way Luke deals with "the poor" in general. The use of the word "poor" is itself an issue. While the majority in the first century lived at a subsistence level, consuming as much as they produced with strong social constraints to keep them "in their place," the Greek word *ptōchoi* signified not the majority, who were "poor" by our standards, but the landless, tradeless, destitute beggars who were "poor" according to their contemporaries. It would probably be best, then, to frame our discussion using "destitute," or "beggar."[29]

Many scholars view Luke 4:16-21 as a foundational, programmatic statement of Luke's christology. Thus the roles of Jesus, proclaiming "good news for the poor" and healing the conditions that cause poverty, are essential to the Lukan portrayal of Jesus. He preserves the many hostile portrayals of the rich and stories of compassion for the poor from Mark while significantly adding to them both with unique material.[30] This makes

[29] See Philip Francis Esler, *Community and Gospel in Luke–Acts: The Social and Political Motivations of Lucan Theology* (New York: Cambridge University Press, 1987) 164–89.

[30] What Luke preserves: Mark 4:19//Luke 8:14; Mark 6:7-13//Luke 9:1-6; Mark 8:36//Luke 9:25; Mark 10:17-22//Luke 18:18-23; Mark 10:23-27//Luke 18:24-27; Mark 10:28-31//Luke 18:28-30; Mark 12:38-40//Luke 20:45-47; Mark 12:41-44//Luke 21:1-4. What Luke alters or augments: he moves Jesus' address in the Nazareth synagogue to the beginning of Jesus' ministry (Mark 6:1-6//Luke 4:16-30); the disciples, including Levi, leave "everything" to follow Jesus (Mark 1:18, 20; 2:14//Luke 5:11; 28); the rich young man is to sell "everything" (Mark 10:21//Luke 18:22); Jesus' followers are to give to "everyone" who asks (Matt 5:42//Luke 6:30). What Luke adds: Luke 1:47-55; 3:10-14; 6:24-6, 34-35; 11:5-8; 12:13-21; 14:12-14; 14:33; 16:1-9; 16:14; 16:19-31; 19:1-10. See Esler, *Community and Gospel,* 165–69.

the differences between the Lukan version and its Markan predecessor all the more curious, since there has been an obvious diminution of the role of the poor in the narrative. The emotional investment of anger, the discussion of the cost of the ointment, its possible use for the relief of the poor, and Jesus' curious point about the prevalence of poverty in human history (Mark 14:4-7; Matt 26:7-12) are lacking in Luke's version, as is John's notice of Judas' penurious motivations (John 12:6).

On the whole, though, Luke demonstrates a particular interest in these beggarly poor, mentioning them ten times in nine passages.[31] Luke receives from Mark the advice to the rich "official" to sell what he has and give it to the poor, followed by the comment on the difficulty the wealthy have in entering heaven (Mark 10:17-22//Matt 19:16-22//Luke 18:18-23) and the passage on the poor widow's mite (Luke 21:1-4). Luke makes this story a condemnation of the extravagance of the Temple by immediately contrasting the widow's offering with the Temple's rich stones and votive offerings (Luke 21:5). He intensifies Mark's advice to the rich man by insisting that he sell *all* that he had, to distribute it to the poor. He clarifies Peter's point, where in Mark he said the disciples had given up everything (Mark 10:29), that he was speaking of their possessions (Luke 18:28). From "Q," and thus shared with Matthew, is the line, "Blessed are you poor because the kingdom of God is yours" (Luke 6:20). Note that Luke does not temper his statement, as does Matthew 5:3, with "poor in spirit." Again from "Q," Luke borrows the observation to John's disciples that "the poor have the good news preached to them" (Luke 7:22//Matt 11:5). Though Luke also shares the parable of the wedding banquet with Matthew, only Luke includes the master's command to bring in "the poor, the crippled, the blind and the lame" (Luke 14:21//Matt 22:9-10). Unique to Luke are the passages concerning Jesus' commissioning to announce good news to the poor (Luke 4:18), the injunction to invite the poor when giving banquets (Luke 14:13), the parable of the rich man and Lazarus (Luke 16:19-31), and the statement of Zacchaeus' intent to give half his possessions to the poor (Luke 19:8). This is balanced by additional material, again unique to Luke, in which Jesus warns against greed and tells a parable of the foolish rich man who mistakenly concluded that life was about possessions (Luke 12:13-21). I suggest that Luke's great concern for the poor is itself the key to understanding that Luke was responsible for the alteration to the text, and why.

We do know that Luke had the opportunity to base 7:36-50 entirely on Mark 14:3-9, but chose not to do so. Instead, Luke apparently chose to

---

[31] Luke 4:18; (6:20); (7:22); 14:13, 21; 16:20, 22; (18:22); 19:8; (21:3).

abandon the discussion of care of the poor and preparation for death in favor of one of repentance, forgiveness, and gratitude. Then it would be most important to determine what motivated him to do so.

The evidence suggests that the alteration of Simon from a leper to a Pharisee may connect 7:36-50 with the preceding pericope.[32] The interpretation of Luke's motivation for this connection will largely depend on the reader's interpretation of Simon's reaction to Jesus. If it is perceived as a rejection, then it could be said that Luke is simply using Simon to extend a contrast in the first passage between Pharisees and tax collectors to a like contrast in Luke 7:36-50 between Pharisees and sinners, in which both tax collectors and sinners accept God's actions through Jesus' ministry while Pharisees, both corporately and individually, did not. It is by no means certain, however, that Luke intends the reader to interpret Simon's reaction negatively. Apart from determining that Jesus was not a prophet, and amicably conversing with him anyway, Luke does not inform the reader of Simon's response to Jesus' teaching. Readers are left to conclude according to their own hunches, which suggests that Simon's reaction is probably not the point for Luke's inclusion of, or alterations to, this narrative.

Lukan Themes Represented

The presence of a theme common to all the gospels in a highly redacted passage may not, in itself, indicate any editorial activity by the redactor. For example, Luke is not unique in demonstrating that Jesus was a prophet. All the gospels attest that Jesus was viewed by his disciples and the people at large as a prophet, something he admitted to himself.[33] So the presence of this theme in 7:39, in itself, does not necessitate Lukan activity. However, there are some other favored Lukan topics in this passage, such as the repentance and forgiveness of sinners, with a depiction of Jesus very purposefully reaching out to seek out and save the lost.[34] The presence of these themes, absent in the parallel texts of the other gospels, presents us with several possibilities to consider. In the first place, it is remotely possible that Luke received a complete tradition of this pericope that already included all of these themes, although that seems a bit convenient. He could also have combined independently received traditions to create the passage

---

[32] Franklin, *Luke: Interpreter of Paul,* 292–93.

[33] The crowds and his disciples consider him a prophet: Mark 6:15; 8:28; Matt 16:14; 21:11, 46; Luke 7:16; 9:8, 19; 24:19; John 6:14; 7:40; 9:17; 4:19. Jesus admits he is a prophet: Mark 6:4; Matt 13:57; Luke 4:24; 13:13; John 4:44.

[34] Luke 5:30-32; 15:1-7, 8-10, 11-32; 18:9-14; 19:2-10.

as we have it now. For example, there is no reason to dismiss the probability that the parable of the debtors existed independently and was combined by Luke with his Markan tradition. It is also possible, however, that Luke was personally responsible for adding these themes to the anointing tradition he received from Mark, precisely because they were among his favored themes.

The most dramatic changes, shifting the focus from waste and the poor to gratitude and repentance, strongly reflect Luke's readily apparent interest in the poor. His tendency was to strengthen, not temper the import of his teachings on poverty and the poor. As a point of fact, there are only two mentions of the very poor in the gospels that are not included in Luke's gospel. In John's gospel those present at the Last Supper misapprehend Judas Iscariot's reason for leaving the meal early, thinking it was to make an offering to the poor (John 13:29). Since this observation is found only in John, we can presume that it was unknown to Luke. We can only speculate whether he would have included it if he knew it. The only other mention of the poor in the gospels that is not included, but was certainly known by him because of its inclusion in Mark, occurs during the meal at the house of Simon the leper, when Jesus responds to the claim that the woman should have been generous with the poor with the statement, "You always have the poor with you, and you are able to do good for them whenever you desire, but you do not always have me" (Mark 14:7). The indifference of this statement, so utterly alien to Luke's deliberate and consistent portrayal of Jesus' concern for the beggarly poor, certainly gave Luke grounds for altering the "inaccurate" depiction of Jesus he found in Mark. On this basis I suggest that the changes are rooted in Lukan themes and understandings of the person of Jesus, and not in a prior source.

CHAPTER FIVE
Interpretation of Luke 7:36-50

Simon's Context or Luke's?

We move now to the question of interpretation. Having analyzed the text's development and spent time diving into the Pharisees and a little into Luke's background, two of several possible cultural avenues of investigation, we need to begin to draw these strands together. The purpose for using our two methodologies, in addition to exposing the reader to new approaches to Scripture, is to obtain a deeper understanding of Luke's text. This purpose requires us to move beyond the analysis of Luke 7:36-50 in its parts and origins, to draw out the implications of our anthropological and redactional research for making sense of this passage as a thing in itself, a self-standing episode in the life of Jesus, and also as a part of a whole, one narrative among many in a gospel. Fundamentally, we need to ask: does it *mean* anything?

The background consciousness created by the negative observations of the Pharisees in the New Testament has played an important, yet regrettable, part in informing our interpretations of their activities wherever they are mentioned. We can see why dictionaries have taken to defining "pharisaic" as hypocritical. Unfortunately, wherever Pharisees appear in Scripture, such as Simon in Luke 7:36-50, some will be inclined to perceive their every motivation and action in a negative light.[1] Thus it should not surprise the reader to learn that there has been considerable discussion and

---

[1] J. P. Louw, "Macro Levels of Meaning in Lk 7:36-50," in J. H. Petzer and P. J. Hartin, eds., *A South African Perspective on the New Testament* (Leiden: Brill, 1986) 132.

disagreement among biblical scholars about how positively or negatively Luke portrays Pharisees.

To put everything into chronological sequence, in Luke 5:17-26 the Pharisees do, indeed, accuse Jesus of blasphemies for forgiving the sins of the paralytic. But they also are necessarily numbered among those who were amazed and gave God glory when that same paralytic picked up his mat and walked away praising God (v. 26). Though they were initially hostile, Jesus seems to have won them over by his healing. Since these Pharisees came from every town in Galilee, Judea, and Jerusalem, an indication of their elevated interest in Jesus, they could spread word of what he had done, even so far as Simon (Luke 5:17).[2]

When the Pharisees next appear, in rapid fire they murmur unhappily about Jesus' choice of dining companions with sinners and tax collectors (Luke 5:30-32), his failure to fast (5:33-39), and the flouting of the Sabbath laws by his disciples, who pick and husk grain to eat on the day of rest (6:1-5). If we step aside from preconceived notions about the Pharisees and their motivations and consider their questions from a first-century Jewish perspective, would we say that their questions for Jesus were unreasonable? In fact, they fit into a religious world where behavior matters and has social consequences. Jesus, as portrayed in Luke, notably without Matthew's vehemence, understands this and answers accordingly. His answers are reasonable enough, even if pointed.

In regard to tax collectors and sinners, who among us, as parents, thinking of drug addicts and the like, would not warn our own children to be careful of the company they keep? Jesus explains, distinguishing between sinners and the righteous, or those who *thought* they were righteous, that his time with tax collectors and sinners was therapeutic, not exculpatory. His efforts were justified only a short time later when even tax collectors began to acknowledge God's righteousness (7:29). Although Jesus' response is not debated further at this point in the narrative, the Pharisees resurrect the issue later in Luke's Gospel (15:1-2), indicating that Jesus had failed to convince them.

If we read Jesus' response to the question of fasting carefully, we will note that he in fact affirmed the practice and pointed to a future time when his disciples, too, would fast, though he also suggested that the times were changing and that old wineskins were inadequate for new wine. Apparently this old observance would have to be understood in a new way or applied for as yet unspecified reasons.

---

[2] Robert C. Tannehill, "Should We Love Simon the Pharisee?" *CurTM* 21 (1994) 429.

The Sabbath question was more serious, since the Sabbath rest was explicitly legislated, carrying the death penalty for willing offenders.[3] Jesus' answer, that the Son of Man was lord of the Sabbath, especially pertinent when the Sabbath rest contravened human need, also fails to satisfy the Pharisees, since in the very next episode they watch, hoping to accuse him if *he* failed to observe the Sabbath (6:6-11). Remember that in 6:1-5 the transgressors were his disciples. The Pharisees became irrational at his healing of the withered hand on the Sabbath, and deliberated among themselves what to do with Jesus (6:11). Their intensity is clearly growing from episode to episode. What began with murmuring has intensified to complete lack of reason, a harsh charge in Luke's rational Greek culture, influenced as it was by the Stoic philosophical movement.

The Pharisees then disappear for a short while from the narrative until, in an aside, the narrator reminds the reader how, by their rejection of John's baptism, they had rejected God's plan for themselves (7:29-30). One may also question, even grammatically, whether the rejection of God's plan for the Pharisees was, for Luke, a once-and-forever summary event, since it occurred at a time preceding Jesus' public activity in Luke's narrative. Having rejected God's plan in one regard, could they no longer accept it in others? Even if the character of the Pharisees never changed as a *group*, does that necessitate, in Luke's mind, that no individual among them could take a separate path? Need the Pharisees as individuals necessarily have been as narratively flat, or without depth of characterization, as the group is portrayed?

After Jesus finished his Sermon on the Plain he journeyed to Capernaum, where he cured the centurion's slave, and then to Nain. There, in an extraordinary act, Jesus resuscitated the widow of Nain's son. For the first time Jesus is proclaimed by others as "a great prophet," which is then reported to all of Judea and its environs. It is at this point, really, that our passage begins to be shaped. It is this report that seems to have drawn both John the Baptist's *and Simon's* attention to Jesus. Remember that Simon hoped that these reports might be true and that Jesus truly might be the prophet.

In response to John the Baptist's emissaries Jesus affirmed his role of healing, proclaiming good news, restoring the dead to life. Thus, Jesus' ministry was at the service of Gentiles and the powerless, and was noticed by the widely acknowledged prophetic figure of John. The narrator then, in an aside, contrasts the acceptance of Jesus' ministry by the people, even the tax collectors, with the rejection of the Pharisees who spurned God's plan

[3] Exod 31:14-17; 35:2; Lev 19:30; 23:3.

for them when they were not baptized by John. This aside in Luke 7:30, just prior to our passage, leads some scholars to conclude that Luke's over-arching approach to Pharisees was no more positive than what we find in Matthew or John.[4] In effect, they serve the narrative simply as antagonists.[5] If this were true, though, then in subsequent passages Luke's Pharisees would be unrelentingly hostile. That does not seem to be the case with Luke's characterization of Simon, though many insist on reading the passage about Jesus' meal in Simon's house in this light.

There is no doubt that Luke wanted us to be conscious of Simon's status as a Pharisee, mentioning it four times, twice affirming that a "Pharisee" invited Jesus to his house (Luke 7:36, 39), and twice stating that Jesus entered the Pharisee's house and reclined to eat (Luke 7:36, 37). In fact, Simon's fourfold identifications as a Pharisee all occur before we learn his name in 7:40. Luke also wanted us to know that the Pharisees, by virtue of their rejection of John's baptism, and thus of God's plan for them, were sinners and thus truly in *need* of Jesus' ministry, which Jesus, in fact, acknowledged by dining with Simon. In Luke 5:29-32 and 15:1-4 the Pharisees show concern that Jesus not only associates with sinners and tax collectors, but eats with them. We are reminded of this phrase in the verses just prior to our passage by Jesus himself, who acknowledges that he has been accused of befriending them and eating with them. The quick juxtaposition of this admission with his acceptance of an invitation to eat at a Pharisee's house suggests both that sharing meals was an integral part of Jesus' ministry to others and that some Pharisees, too, were also "sick," so to speak, and in need of his "physician's" care.

If we quickly conclude either that Simon and his hospitality were rejected as inadequate by Jesus or that Simon dismissed Jesus out of hand, as well as the sinful woman, without taking stock of Jesus' teaching, we, in effect, determine that Jesus' ministry to Simon was also ineffective, a point that, with closer observation, we will note Luke does *not* make. Simon's implicit willingness to consider that Jesus *might* have been the prophet at the beginning of this passage, and his ambiguous silence at the end of it, belying either hostility or disagreement, may be better understood as reflective of hope and reflection, enabling Luke to acknowledge the complexity of the world he knew.[6]

[4] Jack Dean Kingsbury, "The Pharisees in Luke-Acts," in Frans van Segbroeck, ed., *The Four Gospels 1992: Festschrift Frans Neirynck* (Leuven: Leuven University Press, 1992) 1510.

[5] Jack Dean Kingsbury, *Conflict in Luke* (Minneapolis: Fortress, 1991) 21–22.

[6] Contra Kenneth E. Bailey, who considers Simon's evaluation that Jesus was not a prophet, curiously, as contemptuous (*Through Peasant Eyes: More Lucan Parables, Their*

The possibility that Jesus succeeded with Simon is suggested not by Luke's express communication of that option through the narrative, but by his *silence*. At some powerful moments of potential conversion Luke leaves the outcome unspoken, allowing readers to conclude the narrative as they will, perhaps even to consider how they would respond to the circumstances of the story, had they been involved. In Luke, Jesus tells us the powerful parable of the Prodigal Son without ever resolving the question: does the older son enter the banquet or not? We see this again in the testing of Jesus by the lawyer in Luke 10:25-37. When at the end of the parable of the Good Samaritan the lawyer is able to see that it was the Samaritan who *made himself* the neighbor of the robbers' victim, and Jesus says "go and do the same," we are not told if the lawyer does or not (Luke 15:11-32). Just so, Luke's Jesus is able, through a parable, to bring Simon to an awareness of why the woman in the city might love more than Simon does, without ever telling us how Simon responded. The woman in the city, an acknowledged sinner who entered Simon's house, embodied both the centurion who unexpectedly demonstrated remarkable faith and the widow of Nain who, torn by grief and powerless to address her own needs, found comfort in the ministry of Jesus. She exemplified everything that implied that Jesus might bring even Simon to believe. Simon might have heard in Jesus' parable that he, too, was in need of forgiveness, even if his sins were not as public as those of the woman in the city. Luke cleverly leaves it up to us to determine whether Jesus' parable at Simon's table led to Simon's conversion of heart, or not.[7]

Luke apparently knew not only that *some* Pharisees opposed Jesus, but also that some were open to the possibility that Jesus' work might be from God (Acts 5:34-39) and that others had even joined the Christian community (Acts 15:5). Pharisees were not all one thing or the other for Luke. Unlike Matthew, and curiously like John, he saw a middle ground.

The Symposium at the House of a Pharisee

Only Luke includes accounts of Jesus' dining with Pharisees. The activities and discussions at these meals are either unique to Luke or consist, at least in part, of material shared with Matthew, but placed by Matthew in different narrative settings.[8] This suggests that these meals were Luke's

---

Culture and Style [Grand Rapids: Eerdmans, 1980] 11). Simon's tone is disappointed, not contemptuous.

[7] Tannehill, "Should We Love Simon the Pharisee?" 428–29.

[8] Unique to Luke: 14:1-6; from a shared tradition with Matthew, though given distinct narrative settings: Matt 23:13, 23//Luke 11:42, 52.

literary constructions. Such public meals would have provided a familiar setting for material from his sources, reflecting Luke's cultural setting rather than Jesus' or Simon's.[9]

Festive public meals, or *deipna,* and the often inebriating parties, or *symposia,* that followed were common in the ancient Greco-Roman world. Luke included several details that correspond to other ancient literary descriptions of *symposia,* indicating he intended his presumably Gentile, Hellenized audience to interpret the event as such. These include the presence of a number of formally invited guests, a guest of honor (Jesus in this case), and a host, all reclined around a table with hired female "entertainers." An otherwise unremarkable event usually prompts the ensuing conversation and reveals the insight and intelligence of the guest. All these details, including curiously delaying the revelation of the names of the participants, as in the case of Simon, follow the widely attested set pattern of the minor literary form for recounting the notable events and conversations of the formal meal and its *symposium.* Thus some of the curious details of Luke 7:36-50, which some have mistakenly interpreted as signs of conflated traditions, were probably no more than literary conventions that Luke included to set the scene according to the established preset formula.[10]

A similar meal is described in Luke 14:1-24, at the house of an "*important* Pharisee." Such events were more common among eminent and affluent people because of the resources required to entertain in this fashion. Although Luke 7:36-50 does not state outright that Simon is either affluent or a person of public stature, it is implied even by the small detail that Simon would host such an event for the purpose of determining whether his principal guest, whom he knew as little as he apparently knew Jesus, was a prophet.

To the well-informed reader, aware of the many dining restrictions willingly accepted by devout Pharisees, one of the events recounted in Luke 7:36-50 should be jarring. Simon easily determined what kind of woman was present at his *symposium* touching one of his guests in *that* way, and concluded that Jesus could not be a prophet since he permitted her ministrations. Simon did nothing, though, to intervene and stop the contact, which is odd, especially if his conclusion was the same as that of many scholars, that she was a whore. A person whose livelihood was based on sexual congress would have been an obvious source of defilement. His acquiescence to the woman's presence, instead of having her removed,

[9] See also Luke 11:37; 14:1.

[10] E. Springs Steele, "Luke 11:37-54—A Modified Hellenistic Symposium?" *JBL* 103 (1984) 379–94.

even forcibly if necessary, is surprising, not because such behavior was uncommon at *symposia,* which it was not, but because he was a Pharisee with all the Pharisaic insistence on eating meals in a state of ritual purity. We would expect a Pharisee to have her "ushered" from his table and household, which Simon does not do. While we are at it, we might wonder why a Pharisee would invite a wandering preacher with questionable affiliations and associations to that same table.

This oversight forces us to confront three possibilities. (1) Pharisaic practice may have been looser than indicated by all our other sources of information. This is possible, but since it runs against what evidence we do have, even that found elsewhere in Luke's gospel, it is not the most attractive choice.[11]

(2) If our understanding of Pharisaic dining practices is correct, then perhaps Luke was not concerned about the technical accuracy of his reporting. This does not seem likely, though, in light of Luke's concern for accuracy, attested to in his own words and by his consistent, careful corrections of Mark. It seems unlikely that he would have been less than careful about issues of purity if he understood them well. To be clear, he was not strongly interested in these matters either. In fact, of the three synoptic gospel authors he shows the least interest in the fine detail of Jewish observance since, presumably, Luke's audience was not observing them beyond the famous injunctions against idolatry, blood strangulations, and unlawful marriage (Acts 15:29). Thus he often deleted Jewish customs and culture from the received traditions, referring to them only briefly where this was useful to make some other point. Even in Acts, when the controversy over observance of Jewish practices by Gentile converts to Christianity is quite heated, Luke provides only as much detail regarding eating common and unclean foods and male circumcision as was commonly known and commented on by non-Jewish observers in the ancient world, just enough to make the final decision of the early church sensible to the non-observant.[12] Even so, though he was uninterested in cultic purity, Luke was not willing to report inaccuracies. Again, Luke is noted for his "corrections" of his Markan source.

(3) Luke's lack of interest in itself probably points to the third possibility: that he himself was not particularly well informed about the fine particulars of dining practices in the Jewish cultures, let alone among observant Pharisees with their concern about physical contact, sexual or

[11] See Mark 7:1-5//Matt 15:1-2; Luke 11:37-39.
[12] Acts 10:1–11:18; 15:1-31.

otherwise. He was certainly aware of what his sources, both Mark and "L," wrote on the matter, and may even have noted the observances of the conservative Jewish element within Christianity about which he comments in Acts 15:5, but that is not the same as understanding how they live or how their beliefs and observances fit together. Every time I am asked by a Protestant Christian why Catholic Christians worship Mary and the saints I am reminded just how much people can fail to know about each other, even when they are presumably educated and live side by side all their lives.

As already pointed out, all the best evidence suggests that the Pharisees debated complex issues in fine detail to determine appropriate, faithful applications of their ancestral tradition concerning the purity of their food, the vessels in which it was stored and prepared, and the ritual dispositions, clean or unclean, of those who consumed it. If the complexities of the observance were a source of considerable debate within the tradition, what must they have been for the Gentile observer? So even though Luke may have been aware that Pharisees were concerned about ritual washing, he may well not have known much beyond that. Thus we ought to question any presumption that, since the setting for the anointing is ostensibly a formal and apparently public dinner at the house of a Pharisee in Galilee, it accurately reflected a typical festive meal at a Pharisee's home. Again, Luke cannot have represented what he likely did not know well.

In fact, it matters neither if *symposia* were held in Galilee, which seems likely in light of widespread Hellenistic influence, or even if Pharisees would have hosted them and permitted an open door for uninvited guests, which appears improbable. What mattered was what Luke's audience, which was Greco-Roman and Gentile, understood. Thus the appropriate roles and behaviors associated with the characters in the scene, even though it is superficially populated with Galilean Jews, only make sense if they are understood as Greco-Roman hosts, guests, and intruders. In Luke's putative social location *symposia* were known to be quite public and boisterous, and often included the presence of courtesans, who were there to entertain the guests with their conversation, singing, and "other" services.[13] The presence of uninvited females so demonstrably willing to amuse the guests was, in fact, quite acceptable in Greek circles and, presumably, even for those Jews who had comfortably adapted to the customs of the larger Hellenized world around them. It would seem that Luke's Simon was only coincidentally a Pharisee. Perhaps Luke had confused the Pharisees with

---

[13] Judith K. Applegate, "'And She Wet His Feet with Her Tears': A Feminist Interpretation of Luke 7:36-50," in *Escaping Eden: New Feminist Perspectives on the Bible* (New York: New York University Press, 1999) 81.

the patron class of Luke's Greco-Roman world. There would have been no onus for such a figure to excuse a prostitute's presence at the meal, where they would even have been expected. The same applies to the issue of whether Jesus was defiled by the woman's ministrations or not. This concern, which we could hypothesize would have been important to an observant Pharisee, would almost certainly have been irrelevant to Luke's presumed Gentile audience and presumably to Luke himself.

From that perspective Luke's description of the event is quite sensible, explaining other curious aspects of the story. For one, it explains why Jesus was reclining at table rather than sitting, since this was the expected posture for men at these festive meals. The position of the diners, with their heads toward the table and inaccessible to the woman's reach, also explains why the woman anointed Jesus' feet. Though she probably intended to anoint Jesus' head, she arrived too late, after the guests had already taken their places, and she had to settle for his feet, since they would have been the only part of him within reach.

Another area of culturally situated concern for us is the woman's silence. Jesus' failure to dine with her or any other woman in Luke's gospel, or even to engage with her in dialogue, are an ongoing source of concern for contemporary exegetes.[14] We quite rightly want Jesus to behave appropriately, and to show proper twenty-first-century sensitive behavior that is gender affirming and inclusive. Anthropological investigations, though, without needing to either discount or necessarily address how offensive ancient patterns of meaning might seem today, are more concerned with how authors sought to communicate by body posturing, silence, or loquaciousness, and other such activities, to the audiences of their ancient world. Neither Luke nor his audience could have conceived of modern developments of appropriate inclusivity, even though these advances are often supported by scriptural values brought to their fullest implications (e.g., Gal 3:28). That a woman would be silent at such an occasion is noteworthy for other reasons than the ones that first draw our attention, as we will address shortly.

The Woman in the City: What Was Her Sin?

Simon, as a character in this passage, is neither the first nor the last to acknowledge that the woman is "a sinner." Both the narrator (v. 37) and Jesus (v. 47) speak of her sinfulness, even her "many sins." Verse 37, translated literally from the Greek, reads "A woman who was in the city, a sinner,

---

[14] Ibid. 88–90.

learned that he was reclining at table in the Pharisee's house." The narrator of the text is grammatically a bit emphatic about the nature of this woman. Jesus was no less so when he said "her *many* sins have been forgiven."

Because in Luke the narrator has proven reliable throughout, and Jesus, as the LORD's anointed (Luke 4:16-19), is no less so, it would seem an established fact, then, that not only was the woman a sinner; in light of her *many* sins she must have been accomplished in her transgressions. Not that this would have been a problem for Jesus, who was repeatedly accused of consorting with tax collectors and sinners,[15] who readily admitted the tendency,[16] and who knowingly incorporated both tax collectors and sinners into his band of apostles (5:8-10, 27).

We may inquire into the nature of her sin, although this line of thinking has proven to be unproductive for many, especially since Luke does not dwell on it. When a man is called "a sinner" it is hard to know which of the innumerable human failings applies, since all are generally considered possible. For example, when Simon Peter says of himself that he is a "sinful man" it is only vaguely implied that his sin was his weak faith, yet no commentators jump to any prurient conclusions. It is noteworthy, then, when the narrator informs us, in v. 37, that the woman was a sinner, how many commentators quickly conclude that her sin was sexual, that she was a prostitute and ritually impure, an unwelcome guest.[17] Is it not possible that she ignored the dietary laws of Torah, or that she was a vicious gossip, a slanderer at the town well, or a liar? If we work only with what few clues the text offers us, is it not conceivable that she regularly cheated her customers in the marketplace, where she made her living trading rare ointments, offering inferior products and substituting cheap filler in the goods she sold? What does it say about *us* if we jump too quickly to sexual presumptions where women and sin are concerned?

Certainly, the Western church has a long history of attributing prostitution to the woman. In a tragic conflation of all the sources, the woman who was labeled a sinner in Luke, and presumed a prostitute, though Luke never calls her such, has been identified as Mary of Bethany from John's gospel. In a creative leap Western Christianity embraced the popular understanding that Mary of Bethany was the same person as Mary Magdalene, although Magdala, a rural community on the western shore of the Sea of Galilee, between Capernaum and Tiberias, was many miles from the home of Lazarus, Martha, and Mary in Bethany. To state the obvious, Luke

---

[15] 5:29-30; 7:29; 15:1; 19:1-7.
[16] 5:31-32; 7:34.
[17] E.g., Joel Green, *The Gospel of Luke* (Grand Rapids: Eerdmans, 1997) 309.

did *not* associate this woman with Mary Magdalene. Tragically, though, in Western consciousness Mary Magdalene, the generous woman who supported the ministry of Jesus by her presence and her largesse (Matt 27:55-56; Luke 8:1-3), who remained steadfastly with him in his torments when others had fled in fear,[18] the first witness of the resurrection,[19] and the first to proclaim the good news to a waiting world,[20] by a series of misconnections in Scripture became a reformed prostitute. And so it is that Mary Magdalene has so often been depicted in Western art as wearing red, her hair unveiled, and carrying a vial of ointment, none of which is suggested by Scripture. Again one has to wonder what the transmogrification of this great woman, a witness and first evangelizer, into a prostitute says about the cultures that were unable to integrate what Scripture *actually* said about her into their systems of faith and practice.

As for the woman in Luke's account, those who presume a background in prostitution are, admittedly, not without grounds. In favor of their judgment was her willingness to attend a public dinner in the first place. Even more convicting was her act of letting her hair down in front of men who were not of her inner family, an act tantamount to public nudity for a woman who had reached her maiden years.[21] This exposure alone suggested sexual availability, while her actions were inappropriately sensual for a woman of good repute. Even with the relaxed standards at the beach in contemporary America, where skimpy bathing suits are considered suitable attire, the stroking of one person's feet with another person's hair, even simply to dry them, would be considered an erotic act. It is this last act that seems to determine Simon's opinion. Notice, though, that within the world of the narrative Simon does not draw any conclusions about the woman until she lets down her hair to dry her tears. Only then does he construe that she is a sinner, and that any true prophet would recognize her as such (v. 39).

This does, though, pose a different kind of consideration. Prostitutes of the ancient world, as now, most often (almost always?) resorted to this life because of the absence of better options. Being a social pariah, subject to scorn and ostracism, and a receptacle for the passions of strangers and the unattractive, was no more an "opportunity" then than it would be now, regardless of occluded male vanity. Some women, by virtue of their slavery, had this profession decided for them by their owners. Others were reduced

[18] Matt 27:55; Mark 15:40; Luke 23:48-49; John 19:25.
[19] Matt 28:1-6, 9; Mark 16:1-9; Luke 24:1-8; John 20:1.
[20] Matt 28:7-8, 10; Mark 16:10; Luke 24:9-11; John 20:2.
[21] Green, *Gospel of Luke*, 310.

to it by poverty, widowhood, or divorce, and the refusal of fathers or other male guardians to welcome them back. For most, the life would have been a series of miserable exploitations.[22]

In such circumstances, requiring prostitutes to "sin no more," which Jesus noticeably does *not* do here, leaves them without means for survival. What does one do when one's "sin" is also one's only means of support? Even if the presumed extravagance of the alabaster jar of myrrh implied that the woman was an accomplished prostitute, it did not mean that she had sufficient means to survive for any length of time without "working." In such circumstances, we must ask ourselves, how was a prostitute to repent if that meant imprisonment for failure to pay taxes, homelessness, or starvation? Even if successful, this woman in the city was most certainly among the oppressed in need of good news from Jesus.

The possibilities for considering the woman's moral failures in Luke 7:36-50 are more layered and complex than they seem at first glance, though enough so that scholars debate whether it was Luke's intention to imply that the woman was a prostitute at all.[23] For example, we see that in Luke's gospel the older brother of the "prodigal son" accuses his brother of profligately spending his share of his father's estate on prostitutes (Luke 15:30), demonstrating Luke's willingness to discuss prostitution outright. He did not do so in regard to the woman in the city, although he could not have been clearer that she was a sinner, all the while setting up the scene in such a way that Simon would have drawn that conclusion.

To put all of this in perspective, in Luke's Hellenistic environment respected women with social stature did not always eat with their own spouses, let alone attend public meals. While it was possible to eat with one's husband and the closest family members, whenever non-familial male guests dined in a respectable woman's own home she was expected to dine in private with her children in the areas of the home set aside for

---

[22] Luise Schottroff, "Through German and Feminist Eyes," in Athalya Brenner, ed., *The Hebrew Bible in the New Testament* (Sheffield: Sheffield Academic Press, 1996) 334; Kathleen E. Corley, *Private Women, Public Meals: Social Conflict in the Synoptic Tradition* (Peabody, MA: Hendrickson, 1993) 124.

[23] Scholars who suggest that she was not a prostitute: Evelyn R. Thibeaux, "'Known to Be a Sinner': The Narrative Rhetoric of Luke 7:36-50," *BTB* 23 (1993) 155. Joseph Fitzmyer, in a finely shaded reading, suggests that her actions, while perhaps innocent in themselves, gave rise to Simon's, and perhaps the readers', conclusions, enabling the ensuing dialogue (Joseph A. Fitzmyer, *The Gospel According to Luke I–IX* [New York: Doubleday, 1979] 689); Luke Timothy Johnson makes a similar point (*Luke* [Collegeville: The Liturgical Press, 1991] 127). Scholars who suggest that she was a prostitute: Schottroff, "Through German and Feminist Eyes," 334; Green, *Gospel of Luke,* 309; Turid Karlsen Seim, *The Double Message: Patterns of Gender in Luke-Acts* (Nashville: Abingdon, 1994) 90.

women and their work. The festive meal and the *symposium* that followed were considered inappropriate for honorable women altogether. Again, the disreputable women in attendance at these events were there as entertainers to provide music, singing, clever conversation and, often enough, sexual favors.

By the first century, though, these culturally assigned roles were in transition in some areas, apparently as a result of the rapid advance of the empire. Roman culture reluctantly permitted greater latitude for reputable married women to attend public meals in the company of their husbands, and not simply when the meals occurred in their own homes. Though various writers excoriated women for doing so, and made insinuating and slanderous comments about their failures of chastity, we know that it was happening.[24] The very possibility also explains why, in the vaguely parallel anointing stories in the other gospels, there were no "professional" insinuations made about the woman who anointed Jesus on the head in Mark and Matthew, or even of Mary who, in John, also uncovers her hair and anoints Jesus' feet (John 12:3).[25] More importantly, it was this very advance that enabled women to attend the early Christian eucharists.[26]

The repeated reference to the woman's sinfulness, combined with the timing of Simon's estimation of her, just as she uncovers her hair to wipe Jesus' feet, gives us the impression that Simon had drawn a typically *old-fashioned* (for the time) Greek male conclusion about the woman's morals. What Luke intended the sensitive Greco-Roman cultural insider to understand, as the whole story unfolds, however, was perhaps something altogether different, as indicated by the woman's silence.

Though some look upon the woman's silence as appropriate behavior for a Jewish woman, it is unlikely, again, that this meal scene actually reflected Judean culture. As stated earlier, it seems preferable, in light of the clear sign of Luke's editorial involvement in the creation of this narrative, to presume that the woman's silence reflected an element of Luke's culture rather than that of Simon and Jesus in which, when respectable women were audacious enough to appear in public, their silence was expected. Anything else became a sign of poor training and a certain mannishness. This was not the case with prostitutes, who were expected to be verbally

[24] Cicero *Verr.* II.3.68.160.

[25] Contrary to what one might have expected, the presence of a woman at festive Jewish meals, as understood by Palestinian Jews, was apparently more acceptable at this point than in the larger Greco-Roman world, leaving Jewish women particularly suspect of promiscuity by their Gentile neighbors. Corley, *Private Women, Public Meals,* 71.

[26] Ibid. 24–34. See Demosthenes, *In Nearer,* 24; 48; Cornelius Nepos, *Praef.* 6-7; Dio Cass. 57.12; Statius, *Silv.* 1.6.43-5.

entertaining.[27] If the woman had been a prostitute there was no reason for her to have cared for Jesus in such a graphic, attention-getting fashion and not to have spoken to him as well. Her silence suggests that she did *not* have this freedom precisely because she was *not* a prostitute. So how did a woman who was not prostitute end up in this woman's unlikely position?

The best evidence for the woman's occupation is all connected with the circumstantial evidence of her touching of Jesus' feet, her loosened hair, and her lack of a male guardian companion. In fact, Luke seems to have deliberately made the entire course of events appear like an accidental series of actions. Leaving aside the last point for the moment, it seems likely that the woman approached Jesus with the original intent to anoint him, almost certainly on the head. She found him already at table and was distraught because she could not approach or even speak to him in that public setting, and began to cry. Standing as close to him as she could get, behind him and at the far end from his head which was toward the table as he reclined, she literally "rained on" or "drenched" (cf. LXX Psalm 6:7) his feet with her tears. Only Luke, of the four evangelists, mentions the woman's tears. The text does *not* say, in this regard, that she "bathed" his feet, deleting some of the colorful stroking imagery that has fired more than a few misguided conclusions about just what she was attempting to communicate. This was not a sexual overture, but a moment of profound emotion, be it grief, repentance, or even joy. Having nothing else with which to dry his feet, she uses the veil on her head, causing her hair to fall over his feet. Seeing no other access to him, she chooses on the spot to anoint the only part of him she could reach. In an act of utter humility, she begins to fervently kiss his feet. These were certainly rash gestures, which she almost certainly had not planned in quite the way they turned out when she first set out from her own safe place at home. Yet one can see how one event led to the next, in that rational, orderly way Luke so clearly favored.

At this point we could choose between the possibilities that as a reformed prostitute she chose to limit her public speech, or that as a reputable, if sinful, woman (just as there are reputable yet sinful men), she was awkwardly out of her element, stumbling yet determined in her efforts to establish contact with Jesus. While the first is a possibility, it offers only limited utility to Luke's readers, most of whom we should presume were not reformed prostitutes. The second, however, might be very useful in that it addressed the awkwardness of so many of the women who had become attracted to Christianity but found participation in the communal setting of the early eucharists uncomfortably public.

---

[27] Plutarch, *Comp. Lyc. Et Num.* 3.5. See Corley, *Private Women, Public Meals,* 43–44.

Stepping aside from the male preoccupation with matters of sexuality and focusing on how this passage might have been heard, or even read, by first-century women, we might find it more important to focus on an implied inclusivity found in what Luke's text did not say. He did not say what her sin was, allowing any woman who could admit moral weakness to identify with her, regardless of her own personal failings. He did not clarify why, if she was not a widow, she came unescorted by her husband or guardian, allowing women whose husbands were not Christian or observant to identify with her solitary approach to Jesus, and to participate in the Christian communities' gatherings without their spouses. To the frustration of scholars, Luke left it ambiguous whether or not the woman was seeking forgiveness or acknowledging a forgiveness already received, allowing women at any place on the spectrum of repentance and forgiveness to identify with her and seek or express whatever was pertinent to them as individuals.

Luke did clarify that love and gratitude were what drew her from the shadows veiling the first-century Greco-Roman woman's world. I do not think we can understand how this passage was heard unless we can connect with the social reality that this woman, and every other woman who became Christian without her male guardian, but with love and gratitude, made herself subject to misconceptions, like Simon's, concerning her moral integrity.[28] The woman's emotions and tears, oddly juxtaposed with compelling evidence that Luke himself was influenced by Stoicism, seem to have acknowledged how emotionally challenging this could be for some women of Luke's day. One of the most important points of this story may have been for Luke to clarify Jesus' approval of the public risk the woman took to seek out contact and communion with him, and to affirm the many women of the first-century Greco-Roman world who, whether they were widowed or had non-Christian husbands or guardians, recognized their own need for contact with Jesus, and who courageously did what they needed to do to approach him.

It might be good for us to step aside and deal with our own values, our cultural expectations, and their accompanying emotional reactions, especially in connection with the woman's failure to speak for herself. This silence, accompanied by Jesus' willingness to talk about her and to her, but never with her, are a source of disappointment for some contemporary readers, and for obvious reasons: It indicates her subjugation as a woman. There can be no doubt that women *were* oppressed in the first century, as they are to differing degrees throughout the world today. It is disappointing

[28] Ibid. 57.

to many that Luke's Jesus not only did not provide a voice in defense of women in this regard, but by implication seemed quite comfortable and supportive of the *status quo*. Such lack of awareness by Luke is bound to dishearten us, since we so often turn to the Scriptures for moral guidance and support when faced with continuing oppression in our own day. We are not at fault for asking new questions about appropriate roles for men and women or even for feelings of disappointment.

Still, having conceded Luke's strong editorial hand in the composition of this narrative, we—even those of us who accept some level of divine inspiration in Scripture—need to ask ourselves how much enlightenment we can expect of Luke. I doubt that he could even conceive of a world of gender equality.[29] It would seem, though, that he earnestly attempted to address one real difficulty faced by women in his own community, even if the step was a fledgling one in comparison to the much broader encouragement we hoped to find. In this regard Luke's narrative reflected, and in many ways supported, his culture the way it *was,* rather than the way we dream the world could be. Luke may have expected women to be silent, to wait on tables (Luke 4:38-39; 10:40), and perhaps he did not conceive of a ministry for them beyond charitable giving (Luke 8:1-3). In other words, he expected them to be well-bred, docile women of the class to which he himself belonged. It would still be wrong to be too dismissive of what he accomplished here. In his world, before a woman could ever reach the point of being able to speak out she had to know that she was entitled to be present at all.

Regarding Simon

We know that the woman was a sinner because the text so informs us, but by this point it has also clarified that Jesus was comfortable with sinners. To make that very point, just prior to this passage, in 7:34, Jesus himself refers to the accusation that he was a friend of tax collectors and sinners (5:30), and then goes directly to the meal with Simon the Pharisee.[30]

---

[29] For a concise summary of feminist considerations see Sandra M. Schneiders, *The Revelatory Text: Interpreting the New Testament as Sacred Scripture* (San Francisco: HarperSanFrancisco, 1991; new ed. Collegeville: The Liturgical Press, 2000) 180–86.

[30] Corley suggests that Luke carefully edits his material from Mark so that Jesus never actually reclines with sinners or women (*Private Women, Public Meals,* 131–33). Her point is that, while Luke could not deny the tradition he received, he did what he could to soften any presentation that implied Jesus cavorted with Hellenistic lowlife "scum." Her treatment of Luke, while consistent with most presumptions of his social positioning in the upper strata of Greco-Roman society, might not persuade everyone in its treatment of Luke 5:29-30.

We may well ask if Luke intended any irony there. Did Jesus go to dine with Simon to offer assurance and forgiveness to a sinful woman, or to be physician to his host, who was spiritually in need of a doctor (5:31-32)? Proportionality, in fact, suggests the latter. Jesus devotes little time to addressing the woman directly and, at that, only expresses what she already knows, as evidenced by her great love, that her sins are forgiven and that her faith has saved her. He spends, comparatively, much more time with Simon, correcting his misconceptions concerning the woman and the nature of sin and gratitude. This implies that the woman is, in fact, well, or at least recovered, while Simon still needs spiritual therapy.

Jesus' comfort with sinners also explains his willingness to allow this woman to touch him in this quite intimate fashion. Being comfortable with the inappropriate company of sinners, he would not have been put off by their awkward gestures, and would have judged their actions, as in the anointing and drying of his feet, by the intent of the one acting, and not by their social aptness. If *we* are uncomfortable with such actions, then perhaps we can understand why Jesus would have initiated a conversation like the one he had with Simon.

This ought not to be understood as a condemnation of Simon. Jesus never censures Simon for his sins any more than he rebukes the woman for hers. In fact, to the contrary, the immediate movement from Jesus' parable of two sinners incapable of paying off their debts to a comparison of Simon's hospitality to the woman's lavish ministrations suggests that Simon was the man with the lesser debt. In the absence of any mention of particular sins, Simon's condition would seem to have been that of general human sinfulness. Admittedly, some scholars make much of Jesus' comments about Simon's hospitality, but that seems to miss the mark. Jesus did not say that Simon's hospitality was inadequate.[31] Rather, just as the woman's ministrations were, in Jesus' analogy, paralleled by the gratitude of the sinner forgiven five hundred days' wages, so was Simon's hospitality the indication, not of his sin, but of his lesser gratitude, paralleled by that of the debtor forgiven only fifty days' wages. The point was not that Simon was *not* forgiven or could not be forgiven, but that it could be expected that his gratitude, once he was forgiven, would be less than hers. The comparison of the woman's enthusiastic gratitude with Simon's hospitality made that very point.

With Simon we note only the vaguest hint of self-righteousness in his willingness to consider "what kind of woman" was touching Jesus, but this is tempered by the narrator's and Jesus' own frank confession of the

[31] Contra Fitzmyer, *Luke,* 685.

woman's sinfulness. The text does not clarify whether Simon took advantage of the opportunity to repent, but Luke's entire approach to this question would imply that, if he did, he would surely have been as readily forgiven his lesser debt as the woman was her greater one.

Simon's reaction to Jesus' tolerance of the woman's ministrations demonstrates that he had been as open to the possibility that Jesus was a prophet as were the crowds who marveled at his miracles.[32] Again, this was in response to the claim made about Jesus because of his resuscitation of the widow of Nain's son, shortly before in 7:16. Simon's subsequent determination that Jesus was not a prophet was based on his own misevaluation of the woman in the city and her ministrations of Jesus. Let it be noted that to determine someone was not a prophet was in no way a hostile or arrogant judgment. Consider how few people, in fact, have served in this important though rare role in human history. What it *did* do was enable Jesus to demonstrate the precise opposite, that he was indeed a prophet who knew Simon's mind, was familiar with God's will, and could speak prophetic words of forgiveness to the woman.

Jesus, for his part, calls Simon by name, presuming a certain intimacy and absence of malice, also evident in the way Jesus frames the beginning of their dialogue in such a way as to prepare Simon for a respectful disagreement. The use of a name also serves as an invitation to the reader to look upon Simon not as a Pharisee, typical of all other unnamed Pharisees, but as an individual with the capacity to make choices, right as well as wrong.[33]

Simon responds by calling Jesus "Teacher," no mean title in itself. Indeed, within the context of Luke's gospel, with the exception of Luke 20:21 where it is used by chief priests and scribes actively trying to trip him up by *appearing* deferential, "teacher" is normally used respectfully by those who are not Jesus' disciples.[34] In Luke 22:11 Jesus even uses the term about himself. Thus when Jesus says he has something to tell him, and Simon responds unhesitatingly and openly, "Teacher, speak!" we have no reason to presume, even though by this time Simon has concluded that Jesus is not a prophet, that he is to be accorded anything less than deference. The title also prepares the Hellenistic audience to perceive that Jesus

---

[32] Green, *Gospel of Luke,* 307–308. There are some who hold a bleaker opinion of Simon's evaluation of Jesus, e.g., I. J. Du Plessis, "Contextual Aid for an Identity Crisis," in J. H. Petzer and P. J. Hartin, eds., *A South African Perspective on the New Testament* (Leiden: Brill, 1986) 118.

[33] Tannehill, "Should We Love Simon the Pharisee?" 432.

[34] Luke 3:12 (in reference to John the Baptist); 8:49; 9:38; 10:25; 11:45; 12:13; 18:18; 19:39; 20:28, 39; 21:7.

has taken on the role of the learned and wise individual who correctly engages in a brief "Socratic interrogation" of Simon for his edification and understanding.[35]

Again, though Jesus seeks to correct Simon's assumptions about appropriate associations, Simon is not precisely indicted for making judgments of the woman in the city's character, which are only marginally less critical than either Jesus' or the narrator's.[36] If Jesus does offer a more positive interpretation to her actions it is because he understands her motivations, springing from having been forgiven much, and consequently, loving much.

Simon, though unnamed, began this narrative favorably, in spite of his identification as a Pharisee—he was Jesus' host, after all. At the surface Simon was a person of some substance who could invite an itinerant preacher into his house for a meal. If we connect the events of Luke 7:12-17 with Simon's quiet ruminations in 7:39 regarding Jesus' prophetic abilities, we can see Simon's motivation for extending the invitation to Jesus. After Jesus resuscitated the son of the widow of Nain, the public proclamation that "a great prophet was raised up among us" filtered out into the entire region (v. 17). Simon's invitation, following so soon thereafter, implies that he had heard this report and desired to verify it for himself, perhaps even with some sense of messianic hope, although that last point is only weakly supported.[37] Though the reader knows the report to be true, Simon as yet does not, though he is willing to learn the truth and is willing to invite Jesus to his home for that purpose.

Jesus' contrast of Simon's hospitality, or the apparent lack of it, to the woman in the city's abundant gestures has been interpreted by some scholars as an indication that Simon had been rude or at least slighting.[38] It seems to me that this interpretation has been unduly influenced by the

---

[35] E. Springs Steele, "Luke 11:37-54—A Modified Hellenistic Symposium?" 383.

[36] Contra Fitzmyer, *Luke*, 687.

[37] Some early manuscripts of this passage (B* Ξ), although not the most reliable, read, "If this one were *the* prophet, he would know. . . ." This reading is more implicitly messianic than the more reliable "*a* prophet."

[38] Green, *Gospel of Luke,* 308, 312. Ernst R. Wendland, "A Tale of Two Debtors: On the Interaction of Text, Cotext, and Context in a New Testament Dramatic Narrative (Luke 7:36-50)," in David Alan Black et al., eds., *Linguistics and New Testament Interpretation: Essays on Discourse Analysis* (Nashville: Broadman Press, 1992) 108, 110; Judith K. Applegate, "'And She Wet His Feet with Her Tears': A Feminist Interpretation of Luke 7:36-50," in *Escaping Eden: New Feminist Perspectives on the Bible* (New York: New York University Press, 1999) 86; Ben Witherington III, *Women in the Ministry of Jesus: A Study of Jesus' Attitudes to Women and their Roles as Reflected in His Earthly Life* (New York and Cambridge: Cambridge University Press, 1984) 55.

largely negative portrayal of Pharisees, especially in the other gospels. Luke's Jesus was welcomed into a number of households. When he accepted hospitality at Martha and Mary's home, and again at Zacchaeus', there were no mentions of elaborate greeting rituals, just a simple reception by Martha and Zacchaeus (Luke 10:38-42; 19:5-6). Likewise, there was no reference to the greetings at Levi's banquet (Luke 5:29), Jesus' third meal at a Pharisee's house (Luke 14:1), or at Simon Peter's house, although, once healed, Peter's mother-in-law, fulfilling the same role that overwhelmed Martha, waited upon her guests (Luke 4:38-39). We note in Luke 11:37-54 that Jesus' host, again a Pharisee who invited Jesus to dine, marveled that he did not "dip," that is, presumably, wash his hands before the meal, an omission that drew the attention of Pharisees in other gospels as well. Presumably this Pharisee at least made facilities available for the ablutions. Whether Simon, who did not offer water for Jesus to wash his feet (Luke 7:44), offered it in such a way that Jesus could wash his hands, and whether Jesus took him up or not on the water provided, are really not the point of Luke 7:36-50, and are not our concern. It is noteworthy, however, that Luke was at least aware that the custom was observed by Pharisees.

Still, one needs to ask whether there was ever the expectation, in either the broader Hellenistic world or, even in its smaller Judean subdivision, that hosts were to provide water for foot-washing, kisses at the door, or oil for anointing? This is particularly true in regard to foot-washing, where there does not seem to be any indication that the host would wash the feet of his guests. The injunctions to remove one's sandals when on holy ground could suggest either that the sandals were unclean or that the occasion required a worshipful, demonstrable humility.[39] There is no command in Torah requiring foot bathing before entering one's home, but there is also no command that non-priestly Jews need to wash their hands before eating either, and there is evidence that this practice had become common.[40] Rather, in ancient times it would seem that the host might see to it that there were water and bowls for guests who had traveled a long way to wash their own feet.[41] Since there is no indication in this passage that Jesus had journeyed any distance, the courtesy would have been unnecessary.

[39] E.g., Exod 3:5; Josh 5:15.

[40] Mark 7:1-5//Matt 15:1-2; Luke 11:37-38, referring to pre-meal lustrations, does not mention hands, but the use of the word "dip" suggests hands over feet. *M. Yadaim* deals extensively with the issue of hand-washing, but is relatively late.

[41] When the three angels visit Abraham water is offered so that the visitors can wash their own feet (Gen 18:4). In the same way Lot offers water to his two angelic visitors (Gen 19:2), Joseph provides water for his brothers (Gen 43:24), and the old man of Gibeah offers

The record of the Hebrew Bible suggests that kisses were most frequently extended to members of the household and extended family. While
several of the New Testament letters encourage their readers to greet each
other with a holy kiss,[42] the very tendency to offer this encouragement suggests that the practice was unusual and unexpected, reflecting something
new. Now, by entering into the local church, Christians had been united
into a familial relationship. There was nothing in Luke 7:36-50 to suggest
any close affiliation between Jesus and Simon, either because they were
both Jews or because one was the host of the other.

Anointing, for its part, was something one might do for oneself, receive as part of non-ritualistic Hellenistic hygiene at the baths, in a liturgical
reception of an office such as priest or king, or as preparation of a corpse
for burial. There is no reason to presume that anointing was something
expected by guests from their hosts.[43] The woman in the city anointed,
washed, and kissed Jesus' feet while, as Jesus pointed out, Simon failed to
provide water for Jesus to wash *his own* feet, oil for him to anoint *his own*
head, or a kiss to his cheek. If foot-washing, kissing, and anointing were
not expected behaviors, how can we assume that Jesus was shaming Simon
for not doing what may never have been expected? In fact, interpreting
Jesus' statements about what Simon did *not* do as an attack on Simon's
inadequate hospitality weakens the very point that Jesus was making. In
effect, with each of the comparisons Jesus implied, "You did not do the
unusual, but look! She has done the outrageous." The woman's behavior,
which certainly seems excessive to us in the modern world, presumably
seemed at least as much so in the ancient world. *That* was the kind of gratitude she had. *That* was the kind of love that flowed from having been forgiven much. There may be the implication that if Simon and the audience

---

water for the Levite and his wife (Judg 19:21). Similarly, Aaron and his sons had water available in a bronze laver so they could wash their own hands and feet before entering the meeting tent (Gen 30:18-21; Exod 40:31). Conversely, Abigail responds to David's proffer of
marriage by offering to become a slave to wash the feet of David's servants (1 Sam 25:41).
Jesus washes the feet of his disciples (John 13:4-15). It is worth noting that Peter objects and
Jesus offers instruction, in part perhaps because it was not a part of ordinary hospitality for
masters or servants to wash the feet of others.

[42] Rom 16:16; 1 Cor 16:20; 2 Cor 13:12; 1 Thess 5:26; 1 Pet 5:14.

[43] Anointing had more than one purpose, having been used to consecrate priests (Exod
29:7; Lev 8:12; 21:10; Sir 45:15), kings and princes (1 Sam 1:10; 16:13; 1 Kgs 1:39; 2 Kgs
9:3, 6; Ps 45:8; 89:21; Sir 46:13; 48:8; Dan 9:23), prophets (Sir 48:8), and oneself (Jdt 16:7;
Dan 10:3; Amos 6:6). It was also used in a curative fashion (Isa 1:6; Ezek 16:4; Mark 6:13;
Jas 5:14) and as a part of the ritual for cleansing after recovery from leprosy (Lev 14:18, 29).
The particular term used here, *muron,* though having cultic, burial, and festive usages, is not
used in reference to hosts at any point in the Hebrew Scriptures or the New Testament.

were more honest in appreciating how much, in fact, they had been forgiven, their displays of gratitude would be equally excessive, but the thrust
of the parable does not seem to require it. Luke's point was that the woman's
ministrations were beyond the rational, utterly unexpected, exceptional,
and thus meritorious. If the acts of feet-bathing, anointing, and kissing had
been considered ordinary acts for Simon, it would have tempered their
value when performed by the woman of the city, and Luke's point as well.
The evidence suggests that they were beyond all expectation, and thus a
full expression of the woman's great love.

This interpretation brings us to Jesus', and fundamentally Luke's, objective, which was hardly to shame Simon into right behavior. Rather it
was to lead him, and more importantly the reader, to understand several
points: the nature of forgiveness and love, the reality of Jesus' prophetic
role, the risk of hasty judgments, and the superabundance of forgiveness
available for those who are able to acknowledge their many sins. This is
artfully accomplished through the telling of a parable and the engagement
of Simon and the reader in its evaluation. This is persuasion, not condemnation, and Jesus draws upon three concrete examples to accomplish a
change of consciousness: a parable, Simon's hospitality, and the woman in
the city's lavish ministrations. Thus when Jesus asks Simon: "Do you see
this woman?" Jesus is not asking him if he can see the *obvious*, but if he
can see beyond the obvious to what was not so evident, but no less true.
The woman, whom Simon had too quickly summed up as a sinner, had
something to teach Simon about forgiveness and love consistent with
Luke's pattern of demonstrating compassion for sinners, all the while calling them to repentance.[44] According to this model, only the smug come
into judgment.[45]

The Forgiveness of Sins

Jesus, having had several things to say about the woman, never engages her in conversation. He does speak *to* her, though, twice, both times
only briefly, and only at the end of this particular encounter. First he informs her that her sins are forgiven. Remarkably, the first time Jesus for-
gives sins, in Luke 5:21, the scribes and Pharisees ask in protest, "Who is
this who says blasphemies? Who is able to forgive sins except God alone?"
It is noteworthy that Simon's guests, with a yet lingering sense of in-

---

[44] Tannehill, "Should We Love Simon the Pharisee?" 433.
[45] On sinners see Luke 5:20, 29-32; 6:36-42; 7:34, 36-50; 15:1-32; 18:9-14; 19:1-10;
23:34-43; 24:47; Acts 2:38; 5:31; 8:22; 11:18; 17:30; 20:21; 26:20.

credulity, ask the question again, but with less resolve or heat, neglecting this time to include their earlier speculation of blasphemies. Too many miracles have occurred, including the one following their first protest, when Jesus healed the paralytic, instructing him to take up his mat and walk. They may still ask "Who is this . . . ?" but with greater reservation, if not yet faith. For the first-time reader there is still no firm indication that Jesus will or will not succeed in bringing the skeptics among the Jews into a spirit of repentance paralleling the woman's.

Jesus' connection of forgiving sins to salvation follows a Lukan pattern of linking faith with the forgiveness of sins and physical healing. Curing was, itself, a form of salvation in the ancient world before later theological developments tended to reserve the word to describe a particular relationship with God. When Jesus saw the faith of the paralytic's bearers, he forgave the man's sins, and only then went on to cure him (Luke 5:18-26). He was moved by the faith of the centurion to cure his servant (Luke 7:1-10), and by that of the hemorrhaging woman who arranged for her own cure. She, too, was sent off in peace, instructed that her faith had saved her (Luke 8:43-48), as was the one leper, the Samaritan, who returned glorifying God (Luke 17:12-19), and the blind man by the side of the road into Jericho (Luke 18:35-43). Each of these unnamed but forgiven characters, by seeking out Jesus' ministry, made an implicit act of faith, recognizing Jesus' role and acknowledging their dependence on his ministry. Forgiveness, and its resulting peace, were the fruits of their faith in him. All of this accords with Jesus' mission statement, at the beginning of his public ministry, when at Nazareth he proclaimed what it was to be messiah. His anointing from the Spirit of the LORD authorized him to evangelize the poor, announce liberty to the confined, heal the blind, and free the oppressed (Luke 4:16-22).

The pattern of forgiveness, salvation, and sending off in peace was reversed at one miracle when, in a moment of compassion, Jesus returned the son of the widow of Nain to life. She had not sought his healing or, in her grief, expressed faith. She was the beneficiary of unsought kindness. Jesus did not offer her forgiveness or send her and her son off in peace. Jesus' ministry was no less effective in this instance, though, for if it did not flow from the faith of the recipient, it elicited belief in all present, evident in their expressions of praise and their acknowledgment that God had been active in their midst (Luke 7:12-17).

The woman of our passage did not appear to require healing of body, but she certainly needed healing of spirit. As a repentant sinner, whatever the sin, she needed forgiveness and reinclusion in the life of the community. She needed to renew her relationship with God. In this spirit it may not be necessary to determine whether her tears were the expression of sorrow for her moral culpability, the expression of joy for her assured sense of forgiveness, or both. Whether they happened at that very moment or earlier is relatively immaterial in that Luke clarifies by Jesus' reaction that both had happened. Hence Jesus responded, acknowledging her forgiveness, ignoring the resultant questions of the other guests, remarking on her faith, and sending her off in peace.[46]

Conclusion

By carefully examining the similarities and divergences between Luke's narrative in 7:36-50 and the parallel versions found in the other gospels, we have seen how creative Luke was in shaping, at least as seems most probable, an assortment of traditions to create something new that was yet, in Luke's understanding, faithful to the person of Jesus and yet responded to the religious needs of his audience. In this regard Luke was not simply a recording historian, but a creative participant in the process of passing on the early church's reflections on the person and message of Jesus.

In the process of delving into the cultural world of the Pharisees, and recognizing their determined efforts to accommodate their lives to the law of God, we have had to acknowledge their determination to live uprightly. It was their very success at providing a positive religious experience to the bulk of their first-century peers that led some to bring their traditions with them into their Christian communities. By stepping outside the normal polemic summary dismissal of the Pharisees, we were able to reassess Jesus' motivations for dining with Simon the Pharisee. In this case, though, Jesus' interaction with Simon the Pharisee and the forgiven woman who had been a sinner reveals yet another of Luke's typical reversals (Luke 1:46-55). Simon, the upright Pharisee, invites Jesus to dinner, hoping to determine whether Jesus is the prophet people are saying he is. The events and the parable Jesus teaches uncover the unexpected reality that Jesus is, again, dining with sinners just as the Pharisees had accused him of doing. In this case, though, the sinner is not the woman who had been the sinner, but Simon himself, a point demonstrated by Jesus' remark and subsequent parable, a detail Simon does not contest.

---

[46] For a different, but not incompatible, connection of this passage to other acts of faith in the Lukan corpus see John J. Kilgallen, "Forgiveness of Sins (Luke 7:36-50)," *Biblica* 40 (1998) 105–16.

The investigation of the woman's behavior and Simon's response to it suggested that neither of them were simply the Judean characters from the life of Jesus that the text indicates they were. They were as much representative of Luke's own Greco-Roman community, struggling with the judgments made about them or inclined to make such judgments themselves. Luke's parable and teaching challenge the "upright" to inclusivity and humble honesty, and to recognition of their own need for forgiveness and gratitude. Luke's silence about the woman's sin allows all the women of his audience to identify themselves with her as sinners in the city, acknowledging their need for Jesus while struggling with the social awkwardness of attending the early church's public eucharists. Luke affirms their need and invites them all to a meal with Jesus, where forgiveness is offered and great love acknowledged.

BIBLIOGRAPHY

Applegate, Judith K. "'And She Wet His Feet with Her Tears': A Feminist Interpretation of Luke 7:36-50," in Harold C. Washington, Susan Lochrie Graham, and Pamela Thimmes, eds., *Escaping Eden: New Feminist Perspectives on the Bible*. New York: New York University Press, 1999, 69–90.

Asad, Talal. *Genealogies of Religion*. Baltimore: Johns Hopkins University Press, 1993.

Bailey, Kenneth E. *Through Peasant Eyes: More Lucan Parables, Their Culture and Style*. Grand Rapids: Eerdmans, 1980.

Basso, Keith H. "'Speaking with Names': Language and Landscape Among the Western Apache," in George E. Marcus, ed., *Rereading Cultural Anthropology*. Durham, NC: Duke University Press, 1992, 220–51.

Boas, Franz. "The Limitations of the Comparative Method," in idem, *Race, Language and Culture*. New York: Macmillan, 1940 [1896], 273–75.

Booth, Roger P. *Jesus and the Laws of Purity: Tradition History and Legal History in Mark 7*. Sheffield: JSOT Press, 1986.

Bovon, François. *L'Evangile selon Saint Luc, 1–9*. CNT 3a. Geneva: Labor et Fides, 1991.

Brown, Raymond E. *The Gospel According to John: I–XII*. Garden City, NY: Doubleday, 1966.

Chance, John K. "The Anthropology of Honor and Shame: Culture, Values, and Practice," *Semeia* 68 (1994) 139–51.

Chilton, Bruce, and Jacob Neusner. *Judaism in the New Testament: Practices and Beliefs*. New York: Routledge, 1995.

Clifford, James. "On Ethnographic Allegory," in James Clifford and George E. Marcus, eds., *Writing Culture: The Poetics and Politics of Ethnography*. Berkeley, CA: University of California Press, 1986, 98–121.

_____. "Partial Truths," ibid. 1–26.

Cohen, Shaye J. D. *Maccabees to the Mishnah*. Philadelphia: Westminster, 1987.

Corbett, John. "The Pharisaic Revolution and Jesus as Embodied Torah," *SR* 15 (1986) 375–91.

Corley, Kathleen E. *Private Women, Public Meals: Social Conflict in the Synoptic Tradition*. Peabody, MA: Hendrickson, 1993.

Dodd, C. H. *Historical Tradition in the Fourth Gospel*. Cambridge: Cambridge University Press, 1963.

Du Plessis, I. J. "Contextual Aid for an Identity Crisis," in J. H. Petzer and Patrick J. Hartin, eds., *A South African Perspective on the New Testament. Essays by South African New Testament Scholars Presented to Bruce Manning Metzger During His Visit to South Africa in 1985.* Leiden: Brill, 1986, 112–27.

Eilberg-Schwartz, Howard. *The Savage in Judaism: An Anthropology of Israelite Religion and Ancient Judaism.* Indianapolis: Indiana University Press, 1990.

Elliot, John H. *What is Social-Scientific Criticism?* Philadelphia: Fortress, 1993.

Esler, Philip Francis. *Community and Gospel in Luke–Acts: The Social and Political Motivations of Lucan Theology.* New York: Cambridge University Press, 1987.

Fagan, Brian. "Mummy Dearest: A Lost World Emerges From the Sands of Time," *Los Angeles Times,* December 24, 2000, 6–7.

Fitzmyer, Joseph A. *The Gospel According to Luke I–IX.* New York: Doubleday, 1979.

_____. "The Aramaic *Korban* Inscription from Jebel Hallet Et-Turi and Mark 7:11/Mt 15:5," *JBL* 78 (1959) 60–65.

Franklin, Eric. *Luke: Interpreter of Paul, Critic of Matthew.* Sheffield: JSOT Press, 1994.

Geertz, Clifford. *The Interpretation of Cultures.* New York: Basic Books, 1973.

Gillman, Florence Morgan. *Herodias: At Home in that Fox's Den.* Interfaces. Collegeville: Liturgical Press, 2003.

Green, Barbara, et al. *From Earth's Creation to John's Revelation.* Interfaces. Collegeville: Liturgical Press, 2003.

Green, Joel. *The Gospel of Luke.* Grand Rapids: Eerdmans, 1997.

Harrington, Hannah K. *The Impurity Systems of Qumran and the Rabbis.* Atlanta: Scholars, 1993.

Harris, Marvin. *Culture, People, Nature: An Introduction to General Anthropology.* New York: Harper Collins College Publishers, 1993.

Hengel, Martin. *Judaism and Hellenism.* 2 vols. Philadelphia: Fortress, 1974.

Jeremias, Joachim. *Jerusalem in the Time of Jesus.* Philadelphia: Fortress, 1978.

Johnson, Luke Timothy. *The Gospel of Luke.* Collegeville: The Liturgical Press, 1991.

Kilgallen, John J. "A Proposal for Interpreting Luke 7:36-50," *Biblica* 72 (1991) 305–30.

Kingsbury, Jack Dean. *Conflict in Luke.* Minneapolis: Fortress, 1991.

_____. "The Pharisees in Luke-Acts," in Frans van Segbroeck, ed., *The Four Gospels 1992: Festschrift Frans Neirynck.* Leuven: Leuven University Press, 1992, 1497–1512.

Klausner, Joseph. *Jesus of Nazareth: His Life, Times, and Teaching.* Trans. Herbert Danby. New York: Macmillan, 1925.

Louw, J. P. "Macro Levels of Meaning in Lk 7:36-50," in J. H. Petzer and P. J. Hartin, eds., *A South African Perspective on the New Testament: Essays by South African New Testament Scholars presented to Bruce Manning Metzger during his visit to South Africa in 1985,* Leiden: Brill, 1986, 128–35.

Mason, Steve. *Flavius Josephus on the Pharisees*. Boston: Brill Academic Publishers, 1991.

Matthews, Victor, and Don C. Benjamin. "Introduction: Social Sciences and Biblical Studies," *Semeia* 68 (1994) 7–21.

Milgrom, Jacob. "The Laws of Purity of the Temple Scroll," in Lawrence H. Schiffman, ed., *Archaeology and History in the Dead Sea Scrolls*. Sheffield: JSOT Press, 1990, 83–99.

Moore, Jerry D. *Visions of Culture*. Walnut Creek, CA: Alta Mira Press, 1997.

Murphy, Frederick J. *The Religious World of Jesus: An Introduction to Second Temple Palestinian Judaism*. Nashville: Abingdon, 1991.

Neusner, Jacob. *The Idea of Purity in Ancient Israel*. Leiden: Brill, 1973.

_____. *Judaic Law from Jesus to the Mishnah: A Systematic Reply to Professor E. P. Sanders*. Atlanta: Scholars, 1993.

_____. *The Mishna: A New Translation*. New Haven: Yale University Press, 1988.

_____. *Purity in Rabbinic Judaism: A Systematic Account*. Atlanta: Scholars, 1994.

_____. *The Rabbinic Traditions about the Pharisees before 70*. 3 vols. Leiden: Brill, 1971.

Peristiany, J. G., and Julian Pitt-Rivers. *Honor and Grace in Anthropology*. New York and Cambridge: Cambridge University Press, 1992.

Radcliffe-Brown, A. R. "The Comparative Method in Social Anthropology," in Adam Kuper, ed., *The Social Anthropology of Radcliffe-Brown*. London: Routledge & Kegan Paul, 1977, 53–69.

Rohrbaugh, Richard L. *The Social Sciences and New Testament Interpretation*. Peabody, MA: Hendrickson, 1996.

Saldarini, Anthony J. "Pharisees," *Anchor Bible Dictionary*. New York: Doubleday, 1992, 5:289–303.

Sanders, E. P. *Judaism: Practice and Belief, 63 B.C.E.–66 C.E.* Philadelphia: Trinity Press International, 1990.

Schneiders, Sandra M. *The Revelatory Text: Interpreting the New Testament as Sacred Scripture*. San Francisco: HarperSanFrancisco, 1991; new ed. Collegeville: The Liturgical Press, 1999.

Schiffman, Lawrence H. *Sectarian Law in the Dead Sea Scrolls: Courts, Testimony and the Penal Code*. Chico, CA: Scholars, 1983.

Schottroff, Luise. "Through German and Feminist Eyes," in Athalya Brenner, ed., *A Feminist Companion to the Hebrew Bible in the New Testament*. Sheffield: Sheffield Academic Press, 1996, 332–41.

Seim, Turid Karlsen. *The Double Message: Patterns of Gender in Luke-Acts*. Nashville: Abingdon, 1994.

Sievers, Joseph. "Who Were the Pharisees?" in James H. Charlesworth and Loren L. Johns, eds., *Hillel and Jesus: Comparative Studies of Two Major Religious Leaders*. Minneapolis: Fortress, 1997, 138–53.

Simon, Marcel. *Jewish Sects at the Time of Jesus*. Philadelphia: Fortress, 1967.

Steele, E. Springs. "Luke 11:37-54—A Modified Hellenistic Symposium?" *JBL* 103 (1984) 379–94.

Tannehill, Robert C. "Should We Love Simon the Pharisee?" *CurTM* 21 (1994) 424–33.

Thibeaux, Evelyn R. "'Known to Be a Sinner': The Narrative Rhetoric of Luke 7:36-50," *BTB* 23 (1993) 151–60.

Trocmé, Etienne. *The Formation of the Gospel According to Mark*. Trans. Pamela Gaughan. Philadelphia: Westminster, 1975.

Wendland, Ernst R. "A Tale of Two Debtors: On the Interaction of Text, Cotext, and Context in a New Testament Dramatic Narrative (Luke 7:36-50)," in David Alan Black et al., eds., *Linguistics and New Testament Interpretation: Essays on Discourse Analysis*. Nashville: Broadman Press, 1992, 101–43.

Williams, Raymond. *The Country and the City*. New York: Oxford University Press, 1973.

Witherington, Ben III. *Women in the Ministry of Jesus: A Study of Jesus' Attitudes to Women and their Roles as Reflected in His Earthly Life*. New York and Cambridge: Cambridge University Press, 1984.

INDEX OF AUTHORS

INDEX OF BIBLE CITATIONS

INDEX OF TOPICS